Warman's
Fiesta Ware

Identification and Price Guide

Mark F. Moran

©2004 Krause Publications

Published by

An F&W Publications Company

700 East State Street • Iola, WI 54990-0001
715-445-2214 • 888-457-2873
www.krause.com

Our toll-free number to place an order or obtain a free catalog is 800-258-0929.

Library of Congress Catalog Number: 2003112547

ISBN: 0-87349-751-1

Designed by Donna Mummery
Edited by Dennis Thornton

Printed in USA

Words of thanks

This book would not have been possible without the assistance and good wishes of many people, including:

Jim and Jan Van Hoven, Bill and Sliv Carlson, Fred Mutchler, Marv and Deb McNuss, and Ed and Carol Peek.

Contents

On the Road to Fiesta

The Homer Laughlin China Company originated with a two-kiln pottery on the banks of the Ohio River in East Liverpool, Ohio. Built in 1873-74 by Homer Laughlin and his brother, Shakespeare, the firm was first known as the Ohio Valley Pottery, and later Laughlin Bros. Pottery. It was one of the first white-ware plants in the country.

After a tentative beginning, the company was awarded a prize for having the best white-ware at the 1876 Centennial Exposition in Philadelphia.

Under new ownership in 1907, the headquarters and a new 30-kiln plant were built across the Ohio River in Newell, W.Va., the present manufacturing and headquarters location.

In the 1920s, two additions to the Homer Laughlin staff set the stage for the company's greatest success: the Fiesta line.

Dr. Albert V. Bleininger was hired in 1920. A scientist, author, and educator, he oversaw the conversion from bottle kilns to the more efficient tunnel kilns.

In 1927, the company hired designer Frederick Hurten Rhead. A member of a distinguished family of English ceramists, Rhead began to develop the artistic quality of the company's wares, and to experiment with shapes and glazes. In 1935, this work culminated in his designs for the Fiesta line.

Fiesta Colors

Fiesta wares were produced in 14 colors (other than special promotions) from 1936 to 1972. These are usually divided into the "original colors" of Cobalt Blue, Green, Ivory, Red, Turquoise, and Yellow (Cobalt Blue, Green, Red, and Yellow only on the Kitchen Kraft line, introduced in 1939); the "Fifties colors" of Chartreuse, Forest Green, Gray, Medium Green, and Rose; plus the later additions of Casuals, Amberstone, Fiesta Ironstone, and Casualstone ("Coventry") in Antique Gold, Mango Red, and Turf Green; and the Striped, Decal, and Lustre pieces. No Fiesta was produced from 1973 to 1985. The colors that make up the "original" and "Fifties" groups are sometimes referred to as "the standard eleven."

In many pieces, Medium Green is the hardest to find and most expensive Fiesta color.

The Red Scare

During World War II, the U.S. government restricted the use of uranium oxide, which gave Fiesta Red its color. This restriction was not lifted until 1959. Though the company then used a different formulation for the Red glaze, people were still concerned about vintage glazes with even a minute uranium or heavy metal content. The Food and Drug Administration had previously determined that daily use of vintage dinnerware as serving pieces does not pose a hazard, as long as the glazes and decals were properly applied. To be on the safe side, avoid storing food in any vintage pieces, and do not use them in a microwave oven.

Dimensions and Colors

Even though we have provided detailed dimensions for each Fiesta piece, the nature of the machinery used to make each item, and the skill of the potters who applied some details by hand, result in variations throughout the line.

Some glazes also have several shades, to the point that even seasoned collectors and antique dealers may mistake an especially heavy Light Green glaze for the more rare Medium Green. Some glazes are also prone to mottling, including Turquoise and—to a lesser degree—Red. Cobalt Blue and Turf Green pieces tend to show even the slightest scratches more obviously than lighter glazes, and Ivory examples often exhibit cloudy or sooty spots along rims and bases.

And remember that Fiesta colors will also look different depending on the light at hand. Incandescent, fluorescent, and natural light will each add a different color element.

Some bottom marks

Bottom of 6" bread plates in Green, Turquoise, and Yellow, showing "Genuine Fiesta" stamp.

Bottom of No. 1 mixing bowl in Green, showing sagger pin marks, the "Fiesta/HLCo. USA" impressed mark, and the faint "1" size indicator. The impressed size mark on the bottom of the No. 2 mixing bowl in Yellow is too faint to be seen in this image.

Bottom of a teacup saucer in Turquoise, showing the "Genuine Fiesta" stamp. Note the difference in the ring pattern when compared to the Turquoise bread plate.

Vintage
Fiesta Pieces

Ashtrays

Cobalt blue.

Dimensions: 6 1/4" by 1 1/4". Introduced in 1936, and produced through the late 1960s, possibly as late as mid-1969. There are two bottom variations known. Before 1940, the base has seven rings; after 1940, the base has two rings and a "Genuine Fiesta" stamp. Production of Red examples was halted in 1944 and resumed in 1959.

Degree of Difficulty: 1 for all colors other than Medium Green, which ranks 3.

Green.

Red.

Turquoise.

Chartreuse.	$65-$75
Cobalt Blue.	$50-$60
Forest Green.	$85-$95
Green.	$65-$75
Gray.	$80-$90
Ivory.	$50-$60
Medium Green.	$200-$230
Red.	$65-$75
Rose.	$80-$90
Turquoise.	$45-$55
Yellow.	$35-$45

Bowls

Covered onion soup bowl

Covered onion soup
bowl in Yellow.

Dimensions: 6 1/8" by 4 1/2" by 4 3/8" tall with lid. Produced for less than two years, from 1936 to late 1937. Because this piece was discontinued at about the same time that the Turquoise glaze was being introduced, examples in that color are exceedingly rare, and priced accordingly.

Degree of Difficulty: 3 for colors other than Turquoise, which ranks 5+.

Covered onion soup bowl in Ivory.

Covered onion soup bowl in Green.

Cobalt Blue, Green, Ivory, Red, and Yellow. . . . . $700-$750
Turquoise. . . . . $6,000-$8,000

Covered onion soup bowl in Cobalt Blue.

Two covered onion soup bowls and lids in Ivory. The lid on the left is the typical production style with a more flared knob and shorter flange ring; the lid on the right is the early production style and has a more tapered knob and deeper flange ring.

Cream soup cup

Cream soup cup in Turquoise.

Cream soup cup in Red.

Dimensions: 6 5/8" by 5 1/16" by 2 1/4". Produced from 1936 until 1959, the wide C-shaped or "lug" handle is not found on any other Fiesta piece. Bottom marks vary, but all have four rings. Production of Red examples was halted in 1944 and resumed in 1959.

Degree of Difficulty: 1-2 for colors other than Medium Green, which ranks 5.

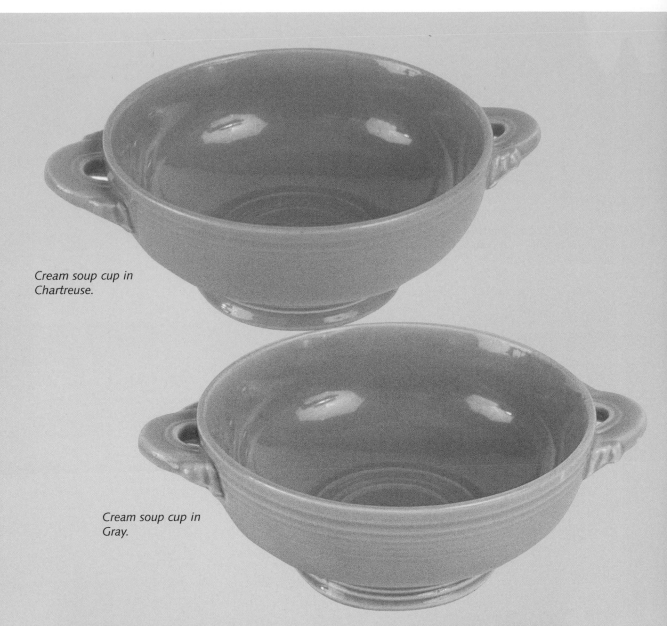

Cream soup cup in Chartreuse.

Cream soup cup in Gray.

Cream soup cup in Ivory.

Cream soup cup in Green.

Cream soup cup in Yellow.

Chartreuse, Cobalt Blue, Forest Green, Gray, Green, Ivory, Red, Rose, Turquoise, and Yellow. . . . . $50-$70

Medium Green. . . . . $5,000+

Dessert bowl

Dessert bowl in six original colors.

Dimensions: 6 1/4" by 1 1/4". Produced from 1936 until late 1960, the pattern inside the bowl may have four or five rings. Production of Red examples was halted in 1944 and resumed in 1959.

Degree of Difficulty: 1-2 for colors other than Medium Green, which ranks 4-5.

Chartreuse, Cobalt Blue, Forest Green, Gray, Green, Ivory, Red, Rose, Turquoise, and Yellow. . $35-$50

Medium Green.
. . . . $700 to $800

Dessert bowl in Medium green.

Dessert bowl in Green.

Dessert bowl in Yellow.

Dessert bowl in Red.

Dessert bowl in Rose.

Dessert bowl in Ivory.

Dessert bowl in Chartreuse.

Dessert bowl in Forest Green.

Dessert bowl in Gray.

Dessert bowl in Cobalt Blue.

Footed salad bowl

Footed salad bowl in Red.

Dimensions: 11 3/8" by 5 1/2". Introduced in 1936 and dropped from the line in 1946, this item was also used for the Tom & Jerry bowl. Variations include interior ring spacing, a foot that can be thick or thin, and either the impressed "Fiesta/HLC USA" mark or the "Genuine Fiesta" stamp. Production of Red examples was halted in 1944.

Degree of Difficulty: 3-4

Footed salad bowl in Ivory.

Footed salad bowl in Yellow.

Footed salad bowl in Cobalt Blue.

Cobalt Blue, Green, Ivory, Red, Turquoise, and Yellow. . . . . $550-$625

4³⁄₄" *Fruit bowl*

Medium green.

Two light green fruit bowls, one 4 3/4" and the other 5 1/2", showing the variation in color intensity and ring patterns.

Dimensions: 4 3/4" by 1 1/2". Produced from late 1937 until mid-1959, these bowls are also marked "Made in USA." The number and size of the rings inside the bowl may vary. Production of Red examples was halted in 1944 and resumed in 1959.

Degree of Difficulty: 1-2 for colors other than Medium Green, which ranks 4-5.

4 3/4" fruit bowls in Chartreuse, Forest Green, Turquoise, Ivory, and Yellow.

Chartreuse, Cobalt Blue, Forest Green, Gray, Green, Ivory, Red, Rose, Turquoise, and Yellow. . . . . $25-$35

Medium Green. . . . . $650-$700

5½" Fruit bowl

5 1/2" fruit bowl in Light Green, left, and Medium Green.

Dimensions: 5 1/2" by 1 3/4". Produced from 1936 until late 1969, early examples—before 1938—have the Fiesta logo and "HLC USA" plus base rings, while later pieces have the logo and "Made in USA" and no rings. Production of Red examples was halted in 1944 and resumed in 1959.

Degree of Difficulty: 1-2 for colors other than Medium Green, which ranks 3.

5 1/2" fruit bowl in Gray.

5 1/2" fruit bowl in Red.

Chartreuse, Cobalt Blue, Forest Green, Gray, Green, Ivory, Red, Rose, Turquoise, and Yellow. . . . . $25-$40

Medium Green. . . . . $70-$80

5 1/2" fruit bowl in Chartreuse.

5 1/2" fruit bowl in Rose.

5 1/2" fruit bowl in Ivory.

5 1/2" fruit bowl in Cobalt Blue.

5 1/2" fruit bowl in Turquoise.

5 1/2" fruit bowl in Red.

5 1/2" fruit bowl in Ivory.

5 1/2" fruit bowl in Yellow.

5 1/2" fruit bowl in Forest Green.

5 1/2" fruit bowl in Gray.

11¾" *Fruit bowl*

11 3/4 in. fruit bowl in Red, with factory flaw.

Dimensions: actually closer to 11 3/8" by 3". Produced from 1937 to 1946, it has two stepped rings under the outside rim. Interior ring patterns vary from tight and even to graduated. All have a bottom mark of "Fiesta/HLC USA." Production of Red examples was halted in 1944.

Degree of Difficulty: 3-4

11 3/4 in. fruit bowl in Ivory.

11 3/4 in. fruit bowl in Green.

Cobalt Blue, Green, Ivory, Red, Turquoise, and Yellow. . . . . $300-$350

Individual salad bowl

Individual salad bowl in Red.

Dimensions: 7 5/8" by 2 3/8". Produced in only four colors for less than 10 years (1959-69), marks include the impressed "Fiesta/Made in USA" or the "Genuine Fiesta" stamp. These are similar to Harlequin bowls, also made by Homer Laughlin, but the Harlequin pieces have no interior rings.

Degree of Difficulty: 2-3

Individual salad bowl in Turquoise.

Individual salad bowl in Yellow.

Medium Green, Red, Turquoise and Yellow. . . . . $100-$150

Individual salad bowl in Medium Green.

Medium Green, Red, Turquoise and Yellow. . . . . $100-$150

Mixing bowl #1 and lid

Complete set of mixing bowls in original colors: Green, Yellow, Turquoise, Cobalt Blue, Red, and Ivory.

Bowl dimension: 3 1/2" by 5". Produced from 1936 to 1944, late in 1942 this size was available only in Red. Bowls made before 1938 have rings inside the bottom, and are usually marked "Fiesta/HLC USA" and the size number. Bowls made later have no rings and are usually marked "Fiesta/Made in USA" and the size number.

Mixing Bowl Lid #1: 5 1/8" diameter. Some sources believe they were produced for less than six months in 1936-37. Condition—though still important—is less of a factor because of their rarity.

Degree of Difficulty: Bowls, 3-4; Lids, 5.

No. 1 and 2 mixing bowls in Green and Yellow.

No. 1 mixing bowl in Red, with an Ivory lid.

Bowl: Cobalt Blue, Green, Ivory, Red, Turquoise, and Yellow.
. . . . $250-$325

Lid: Cobalt Blue, Green, Ivory, Red, Turquoise, and Yellow
. . . . $650-$750

Mixing bowl #2 and lid

No. 2 mixing bowl in Turquoise with a Cobalt Blue lid.

Bowl dimension: 4" by 5 7/8". Produced from 1936 to 1944, late in 1942 this size was available only in Yellow. Bowls made before 1938 have rings inside the bottom, and are usually marked "Fiesta/HLC USA." Bowls made later have no rings and are usually marked "Fiesta/Made in USA."

Mixing Bowl Lid #2: 6 1/8" diameter: Some sources believe they were produced for less than six months in 1936-37. Condition—though still important—is less of a factor because of their rarity.

Degree of Difficulty: Bowls, 2-3; Lids, 5.

Bowl: Cobalt Blue, Green, Ivory, Red, Turquoise, and Yellow.
. . . . $110-$160
Lid: Cobalt Blue, Green, Ivory, Red, Turquoise, and Yellow. $750-$800

Mixing bowl #3 and lid

No. 3 mixing bowl in Yellow.

Bowl dimension: 4 1/2" by 6 3/4". Produced from 1936 to 1944, late in 1942 this size was available only in Green. Bowls made before 1938 have rings inside the bottom, and are usually marked "Fiesta/HLC USA." Bowls made later have no rings and are usually marked "Fiesta/Made in USA."

Mixing Bowl Lid #3: about 7" diameter. Some sources believe they were produced for less than six months in 1936-37. Condition—though still important—is less of a factor because of their rarity.

Degree of Difficulty: Bowls, 2-3; Lids, 5.

Bowl: Cobalt Blue, Green, Ivory, Red, Turquoise, and Yellow. $135-$170

Lid: Cobalt Blue, Green, Red, Turquoise, and Yellow. . . . . $750-$800
Ivory. . . . . . . $900-$950

No. 3 mixing bowl and lid in Yellow.

No. 3 mixing bowl and lid in Cobalt Blue.

Mixing bowl #4 and lid

No. 4 mixing bowl in Cobalt Blue.

Bowl dimension: 5" by 7 3/4". Produced from 1936 to 1944, late in 1942 this size was available only in Ivory. Bowls made before 1938 have rings inside the bottom, and are usually marked "Fiesta/HLC USA" and the size number. Bowls made later have no rings and are usually marked "Fiesta/Made in USA" and the size number.

Mixing Bowl Lid #4: 7 7/8". diameter. Some sources believe they were produced for less than six months in 1936-37. Condition—though still important—is less of a factor because of their rarity.

Degree of Difficulty: Bowls, 2-3; Lids, 5.

Bowls:
Cobalt Blue. $200-$225
Green. . . . . . $100-$120
Ivory. . . . . . . $150-$200
Red. . . . . $200-$225
Turquoise. . . $150-$175
Yellow. . . . . . $110-$140

Lids: Cobalt Blue, Green, Ivory, Red, Turquoise, and Yellow.
. . . . . . $1,000-$1,200

No. 4 mixing bowl in Ivory.

No. 1 mixing bowl lid in Green and a No. 4 mixing bowl lid in Red.

Mixing bowl #5 and lid

Bowl dimensions: 5 3/4" by 8 1/2". Produced from 1936 to 1944, late in 1942 this size was available only in Yellow. Bowls made before 1938 have rings inside the bottom, and are usually marked "Fiesta/HLC USA" and the size number. Bowls made later have no rings and are usually marked "Fiesta/Made in USA" and the size number.

Mixing Bowl Lid #5: A few were made as a trial run, but they were never put into production.

Degree of Difficulty: Bowls, 2-3; Lids, 5++.

Bowls: Cobalt Blue, Green, Ivory, Red, Turquoise, and Yellow.
. . . . **$225 to $270**

Lids: Green and Red. . . . . **$11,000-$13,000**

Mixing bowl #6 and lid

No. 6 mixing bowl in Red.

Bowl dimensions: 6 1/4" by 9 3/4". Produced from 1936 to 1944, late in 1942 this size was available only in Turquoise. Bowls made before 1938 have rings inside the bottom, and are usually marked "Fiesta/HLC USA" and the size number. Bowls made later have no rings and are usually marked "Fiesta/Made in USA" and the size number.

Mixing Bowl Lid #6: A few were made as a trial run, but they were never put into production.

Degree of Difficulty: Bowls, 3-4; Lids, 5++.

Lids:
Green. $11,000
Red. $14,000+

Bowls:
Cobalt Blue, Green, Ivory, Red,
Turquoise and Yellow . .$300 to $375

Mixing bowl #7

No. 7 mixing bowl in Ivory.

Bowl dimensions: 7 1/8" by 11". Produced from 1936 to 1944, late in 1942 this size was available only in Cobalt Blue. Bowls made before 1938 have rings inside the bottom, and are usually marked "Fiesta/HLC USA" and the size number. Bowls made later have no rings and are usually marked with "Fiesta/Made in USA" and the size number. There are no known lids for this size bowl.

Degree of Difficulty: 3-4.

No. 7 mixing bowl in Cobalt Blue.

Cobalt Blue, Green, Ivory, Red, Turquoise, and Yellow. . . . . **$550-$650**

8½ in. Nappy

Nappy in Turquoise.

Technically, nappy refers to a rimless, shallow bowl, but the term has always been applied to this piece and the next larger size. From a total of 75 items, this size is one of only 14 Fiesta pieces that were produced for more than 33 years, from 1936 to 1969. Impressed marks include "Fiesta/HLC USA" before 1938, and "Fiesta/Made in USA" after 1938. Production of Red examples was halted in 1944 and resumed in 1959.

Degree of Difficulty: 1-2 for all colors other than Medium Green, which ranks 3-4.

8 1/2" nappy in Green.

8 1/2" nappy in Ivory, with faint spots of sooty discoloration around the rim typical of pieces in this color.

8 1/2" nappy in Ivory.

8 1/2" nappy in Cobalt Blue.

8 1/2" nappy in Turquoise.

8 1/2" nappy in Red.

8 1/2" nappy in Rose.

Chartreuse, Cobalt Blue, Forest Green, Gray, Green, Ivory, Red, Rose, Turquoise, and Yellow. . . . . $40-$65
Medium Green. . . . . $150-$175

8 1/2" nappy in Gray.

8 1/2" nappy in Yellow.

8 1/2" nappy in Chartreuse.

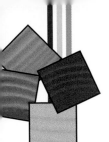

9½ in. Nappy

9 1/2" nappy in Ivory.

Technically, nappy refers to a rimless, shallow bowl, but the term has always been applied to this piece and the next smaller size. One of the original items introduced in 1936, this size is one of 14 Fiesta pieces that were dropped from the line in 1946. Impressed marks include "Fiesta/HLC USA" (two sizes) before 1938, and "Fiesta/Made in USA" after 1938. Production of Red examples was halted in 1944.

Degree of Difficulty: 2-3

Cobalt Blue, Green,
Ivory, Red, Turquoise,
and Yellow. . $55-$70

9 1/2" nappy in Red.

Unlisted or promotional salad bowl

Unlisted salad bowl in Yellow.

Dimensions: 9 3/4" by 3 1/2". Made as part of a three-piece set for less than three years, from 1940 to 1943, there are no interior rings on the bowls, and the impressed mark is "Fiesta/Made in USA/HLCo." Rarely found with the fork and spoon (**$300 to $400/pair**), which were part of the Fiesta Kitchen Kraft line (see Kitchen Kraft).

Degree of Difficulty: 2-3 for Yellow, 4-5 for other colors.

Cobalt Blue. . . . $1,700-$1,750
Ivory and Red. . $2,300-$2,400

Yellow. . . . . $100-$125

Candleholders

Bulb candleholders

Bulb candleholders in Turquoise (note color variation).

Dimensions: 3 3/4" by 2 1/2". Made for 11 years, from 1936 until 1946, this is another Fiesta item that has become an icon of the line. Red was discontinued in 1944. They are marked inside the base "Fiesta HLCo USA."

Degree of Difficulty: 1-2

Cobalt Blue, Green, Ivory, Red, Turquoise, and Yellow. . $90-$125/pair

Tripod candleholders

Tripod candleholders in Ivory and Yellow.

Dimensions: 3 1/2" by 4 1/2". With their complex buttressed columns, these were produced for seven years, from 1935 to 1942, but they are also part of the Post-'86 wares. The early versions are marked with an impressed "Fiesta/HLC USA." One way to tell a vintage holder from a new one (other than the color range) is that almost all early holders have a completely glazed base, called a "wet foot." New holders have the glaze wiped from the base.

Degree of Difficulty: 3-4

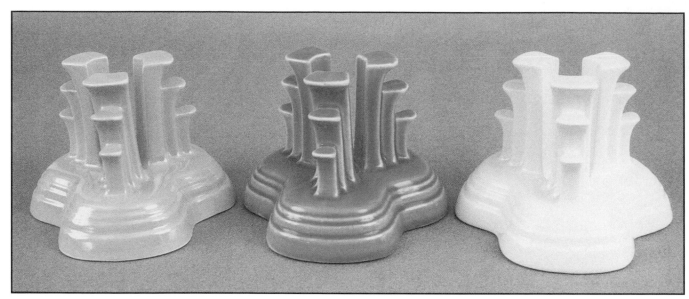

Tripod candleholders in Yellow, Green, and Ivory.

Tripod candleholders in Cobalt Blue and Red.

Cobalt Blue. . . . . $650-$700/pair
Green. . . . . $475-$525/pair
Ivory. . . . . $600-$650/pair
Red and Turquoise. . . . . $675-$725/pair
Yellow. . . . . $400-$425/pair

Carafe

Carafe in Turquoise.

Dimensions: 9 1/4" by 7 1/8" by 6 1/8". Made from 1935 to 1946, the carafe is an icon of the Fiesta line. Red was discontinued in 1944. It is marked with an impressed "Fiesta/HLC USA."

Degree of Difficulty: 2-3

Cobalt Blue, Green, Ivory, Red,
Turquoise and Yellow. . $225-$325

Carafe in Yellow.

Carafe in Cobalt Blue.

Carafe in Red.

Carafe in Green.

Carafe in Ivory.

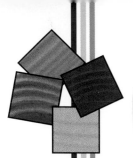

Casseroles

Covered casserole

Covered casserole in Turquoise.

Dimensions: 9 3/4" by 7 7/8" by 5 3/4" tall with lid. Produced from 1935 until 1969, it has two impressed marks: "Fiesta/HLC USA" and the later "Fiesta/Made in USA." Production of Red examples was halted in 1944 and resumed in 1959.

Degree of Difficulty: 2-3

Covered casserole in Red.

Covered casserole in Red.

Chartreuse.	$300-$325	Green.	$150-$175
Cobalt Blue.	$250-$275	Ivory and Red.	$250-$300
Forest Green and Gray.	$300-$325		

Covered casserole in Ivory.

Covered casserole in Medium Green.

Medium Green. . . . . . . $1,600-$1,700

Covered casserole in Rose.

Covered casserole in Yellow.

Rose. . . . . $300-$325   Yellow. . . . . $150-$175
Turquoise. . . . . $160-$180

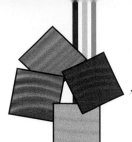

French casserole

French casserole in Yellow.

Dimensions: 11 7/8" by 8 3/8" by 4 1/4" with lid. This was a special promotion item, produced from 1940 until 1943. Examples with lids are very rare, as are colors other than Yellow. Marked "Fiesta/Made in USA."

Degree of Difficulty: 3-4 in colors other than Yellow.

Cobalt Blue. . . . . $3,550-$3,650
Green. . . . . $575-$625

Ivory. . . . . $525-$575
Yellow. . . . . $275-$325

Promotional casserole

Kitchen Kraft covered casserole with Fiesta Red lid and Fiesta Green bowl on a Fiesta Yellow Kitchen Kraft 9 1/2" pie plate. This set in the same color combination also sold by Royal Metal Manufacturing.

Part of the Kitchen Set, dimensions: 8 1/8" diameter (bowl lid) by 4 1/4" tall, plate 9 1/2" diameter. This set from 1942 features the Kitchen Kraft covered casserole with Fiesta Red lid and Fiesta Green bowl on an unmarked Fiesta Yellow Kitchen Kraft 9 1/2" pie plate.

Degree of Difficulty: 2-3

Cobalt Blue, Green, Ivory, Red, Turquoise and Yellow. . . . . **$150-$175/set**

Coffeepots

Coffeepot in Cobalt Blue.

Dimensions: 10 3/8" by 8" by 4 1/2" (lid). Produced from 1935 to 1959, it held seven cups and can be marked "Fiesta/HLC USA" or "Fiesta/Made in USA." Red was discontinued in 1944; examples in Gray bring a premium.

Degree of Difficulty: 2-3 for colors other than Gray, which ranks 4-5.

Coffeepot in Red.

Chartreuse. . . . . $325-$350
Cobalt Blue. . . . . . . $250-$300
Forest Green. . . . . . $325-$350
Gray. . . . . $675-$725
Green. . . . . $225-$250
Ivory. . . . . $225-$250
Red. . . . . $275-$325
Rose. . . . . $375-$425
Turquoise. . . . . $160-$180
Yellow. . . . . $200-$250

Coffeepot in Turquoise.

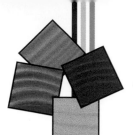

Demitasse coffeepot

Demitasse coffeepot and cups and saucers in original colors.

Also called "After Dinner" or "A.D.," dimensions: 7 5/8" by 6 7/8" by 3 1/2" (lid). Produced from 1935 until 1942, some lids have small steam holes. It is marked "Fiesta/HLC USA."

Degree of Difficulty: 3-4.

Cobalt Blue. . . . . $600-$625
Green. . . . . $675-$725
Ivory. . . . . $625-$650
Red and Turquoise. . . $700-$725
Yellow. . . . . $400-$425

Demitasse coffeepot in Green.

Demitasse coffeepots in Turquoise and Red.

Comports

Comport

Comport in Cobalt Blue.

Comport in Ivory.

Called the 12" comport, dimensions: 12 3/8" by 3 3/8". Produced from 1935 to 1946, these comports may be found unmarked or with a "Genuine Fiesta" stamp. Production of Red examples was halted in 1944.

Degree of Difficulty: 2-3

Cobalt Blue. . . . . $200-$225
Green. . . . . $150-$175
Ivory. . . . . $200-$225

Red and Turquoise. . . . . . . $700-$725
Yellow. . . . . $400-$425

Sweets comport

Sweets comport in Cobalt Blue.

Sweets comport in Yellow.

Dimensions: 5 1/8" by 3 1/2". Produced from 1936 to 1946, these pieces may be found with a "HLCo USA" stamp, but they are seldom marked. Production of Red examples was halted in 1944.

Degree of Difficulty: 1-2

Cobalt Blue, Green, Ivory, Red, Turquoise, and Yellow. . . . **$75 to $110**

Creamers

Creamer, sugar, tray set

Individual creamer and sugar in Yellow with Cobalt Blue figure-8 tray.

This four-piece set was a special promotion, made from 1940 until 1943, and the creamer and sugar shapes are markedly different from the earlier stick-, scroll-, and ring-handle versions, and the later C-handle style. The standard color combination was Cobalt Blue for the tray (stamped "Genuine Fiesta"), and Yellow for the creamer and sugar (impressed "Made in USA"). But other colors, chiefly Red and Turquoise, have been found. Most Cobalt Blue trays will often show even the slightest surface scratching, as do all pieces in this glaze. Check sugar bowl lids for rim chips.

Creamer (called "the individual"), 4 7/8" by 2 5/8" by 3 5/8".

Sugar Bowl (called "the individual"), 5 1/4" by 3 1/2" by 3 5/8".

Tray (figure-8), 10 3/8" by 5" by 7/8".

Degree of Difficulty: 2-3 for the standard Cobalt and Yellow combination, 3-4 for Turquoise and Red.

Individual creamer (Red) and sugar (Yellow) on a Turquoise figure-8 tray.

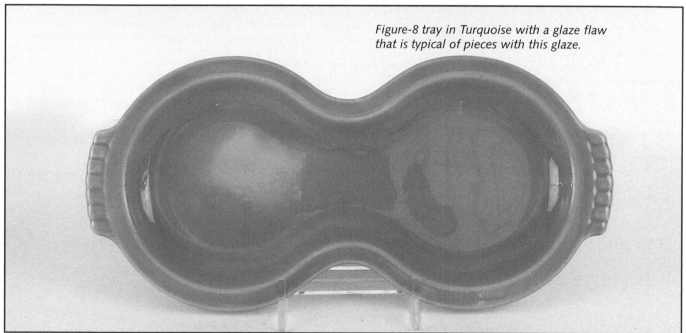

Figure-8 tray in Turquoise with a glaze flaw that is typical of pieces with this glaze.

Creamers:
Red. . . . . $350-$400
Turquoise. . . . . $4,700-$5,000
Yellow. . . . . $80-$100

Sugar Bowls:
Red and Turquoise. . . . . . . $400-$425
Yellow. . . . . $175-$225

Trays:
Cobalt Blue. . . . . $100-$150
Turquoise and Yellow. . . . $500-$600

Ring-handle creamer

Ring-handle creamer in Medium Green (with covered sugar).

Dimensions: 5 7/8" by 3" by 3 5/8". Produced from 1938 until 1969, the ring-handle creamer replaced the stick handle. Production of Red examples was halted in 1944 and resumed in 1959.

Degree of Difficulty: 1-2 depending on color.

Chartreuse, Cobalt Blue, Forest Green, Gray, Green, Ivory, Red, Rose, Turquoise, and Yellow. . . . . $25-$40

Medium Green. . . . . $125-$150

Ring-handle creamer in Green.

Ring-handle creamer in Rose.

Ring-handle creamer in Turquoise.

Stick-handle creamer

Stick-handle creamer in Ivory.

Stick-handle creamer in Yellow.

Dimensions: 4 5/8" by 3" by 3 5/8" without handle. Produced from 1935 until 1938, it was succeeded by the more versatile ring-handle creamer. It bears an impressed "HLC USA" mark.

Degree of Difficulty: 2-3 for colors other than Turquoise, which ranks 3-4.

Cobalt Blue.	$60-$65	Red.	$55-$65
Green.	$35-$45	Turquoise.	$100-$125
Ivory.	$55-$65	Yellow.	$35-$45

Cups
Egg cup

Egg cup in Turquoise.

Dimensions: 3 3/8" by 3 1/8". The egg cup was added to the Fiesta line in 1936, and was produced until 1959. Often unmarked, it can also have a "Made in USA" impressed mark. Production of Red examples was halted in 1944.

Degree of Difficulty: 2-3 for the original six colors, 3-4 for Fifties colors.

Chartreuse. . . . . $125-$175	Ivory. . . . . $85-$95
Cobalt Blue. . . . . $60-$70	Red. . . . . $100-$125
Forest Green. . . . . $125-$175	Rose. . . . . $400-$450
Gray. . . . . $500-$550	Turquoise. . . . . $90-$100
Green. . . . . $70-$80	Yellow. . . . . $70-$80

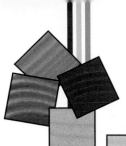

Demitasse cup and saucer

Demitasse cups and saucers in Cobalt Blue and Turquoise.

Also called "After Dinner" or "A.D." Dimensions: Cup, 2 1/2" without handle by 2 1/2", and saucer, 5 1/4" diameter. These cups are rarely marked, and they also vary in style details: Cups made before late 1937 have a flat inner bottom; those made after that time have a rounded inner bottom. Early demitasse saucers also have two rings around the base or foot; examples after 1937 have a single ring and are usually stamped "Genuine Fiesta." Cups and saucers were made until about 1958, but production of Red examples was halted in 1944.

Degree of Difficulty: 2-3 for the original six colors, 3-4 for Fifties colors.

Chartreuse. . . . .$500-$550/**pair**	Ivory. . . . . $85-$95/**pair**
Cobalt Blue. . . . . $100-$110/**pair**	Red. . . . . $100-$125/**pair**
Forest Green. . . . . . . $400-$450/**pair**	Rose. . . . . $400-$450/**pair**
Gray. . . . . $500-$550/**pair**	Turquoise. . . . . $90-$100/**pair**
Green. . . . . $70-$80/**pair**	Yellow. . . . . $70-$80/**pair**

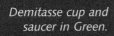

Demitasse cup and saucer in Yellow.

Demitasse cups and saucers in Green and Yellow.

Demitasse cups and saucers in Ivory and Red.

Teacup and saucer

Teacup and saucer in Medium Green.

Dimensions: Cup, 3 3/8" without handle by 2 7/8", and saucer, 6 1/8" diameter. Made from 1936 to 1969, the teacup and saucer come in three variations: Cups made up to 1937 have a flat inner bottom and rings inside the rim; saucers have five rings around the base or foot; neither is marked. Cups made after 1937 have a rounded inner bottom and inner rim rings, while the saucers have a single wide ring under the rim, and a "Genuine Fiesta" stamp. In the 1960s, the cup was slightly enlarged and redesigned without a turned foot or rings inside the rim; the saucers are slightly deeper with a double band of rings under the rim, and a "Genuine Fiesta" stamp.

Degree of Difficulty: 1-2 for the later version, 3-4 for the earlier version.

Teacup and saucer in Forest Green.

Teacup and saucer in Gray.

Chartreuse, Cobalt Blue, Forest Green, Gray, Green, Ivory, Red, Rose,
   Turquoise, and Yellow. . . . . $30-$45/**pair**
Medium Green. . . . . $70-$80/**pair**

Teacup and saucer in Rose.

Teacup and saucer in Cobalt Blue.

Teacup and saucer in Yellow.

Teacup and saucer in Ivory.

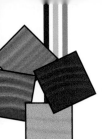

Marmalade jar

Marmalades in Red and Yellow, including glass spoons with colored tips.

Dimensions: 3 7/8" by 4 1/2" with lid. Made from 1936 to 1946, these are marked on the base "Fiesta/HLC USA." Production of Red examples was halted in 1944.

Degree of Difficulty: 3-4

Cobalt Blue, Green, Ivory, Red, Turquoise, and Yellow. . . . . $300-$400

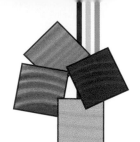

Mugs

Tom & Jerry mug

Tom & Jerry mugs in the original six colors.

Dimensions: 3 1/8" by 3 1/8" by 4 3/8". Produced from 1936 until 1969, it is one of only two items in the Fiesta line that has no ring decoration on the body. In addition to the 11 standard colors, it also comes in Ivory with gold lettering and trim for use with a set that includes the footed salad bowl converted to holiday beverage use. When marked, the mugs bear the "Genuine Fiesta" stamp. Production of Red examples was halted in 1944 and resumed in 1959.

Degree of Difficulty: 1-2

Tom & Jerry mug in Medium Green.

Chartreuse and Cobalt Blue.	$80-$90
Forest Green.	$75-$85
Gray.	$70-$80
Green.	$55-$65
Ivory.	$65-$75
Medium Green.	$115-$125
Red.	$70-$80
Rose.	$75-$85
Turquoise.	$40-$50
Yellow.	$40-$50

Three Tom & Jerry mugs in Yellow, Green, and Red.

Three Tom & Jerry mugs in Forest Green, Gray, and Chartreuse.

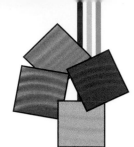

Mustard jar
Covered mustard

Three mustards in Yellow, Green, and Turquoise.

Two mustards in Red and Ivory.

Dimensions: 2 1/2" by 3 1/8" with lid. Produced from 1936 to 1946, it is rarely marked. Production of Red examples was halted in 1944. It is easily distinguished from the covered marmalade jar by its smaller size and the tapered—rather than flaring—knob on the lid.

Degree of Difficulty: 3-4

Cobalt Blue, Green, Ivory, Red, Turquoise, and Yellow. . . . . $300-$375

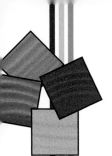

Pitchers

Disk juice pitcher

Disk juice pitcher in Harlequin Yellow, and six juice tumblers in Fiesta Yellow, Turquoise, Red, Cobalt Blue, Ivory, and Green.

Dimensions: 6" by 6 1/2" by 3 1/2". Produced from 1939 until 1943, it was also made for special promotions in 1948 (called "Jubilee" and featuring a palette of Celadon Green, Pink, Gray, and Beige) and 1951 (for the Woolworth's "Rhythm" line that included Harlequin Yellow), and was part of a seven-piece set that included six tumblers in standard colors. Usually marked "Fiesta/Made in USA."

Degree of Difficulty: 1 for Yellow versions, 3-4 for Red, 5+ for other colors.

Three disk juice pitchers: left, Fiesta Yellow; center, Post-'86 Yellow; right, Harlequin Yellow; and a mini disk pitcher in Post-'86 Sunflower.

Gray. . . . . $3,000+   Turquoise. . . . . $10,000+
Red. . . . . $600-$700   Fiesta and Harlequin Yellow. . $40-$50

Disk water pitcher

Disk water pitchers, right, in vintage Red; left, in Post-'86 Persimmon.

Dimensions: 7 1/2" by 8 3/4" by 5". Made from 1938 to 1969, this pitcher is the piece that most collectors identify as being quintessentially Fiesta. It is also part of the Post-'86 line in contemporary colors. Production of Red examples was halted in 1944 and resumed in 1959. Pitchers by other manufacturers in this shape are common, so look for the "Fiesta/Made in USA" impressed mark.

Degree of Difficulty: 1-2 for original colors, 3-4 for Fifties colors, 4-5 for Medium Green.

Chartreuse.	$250-$300	Green.	$100-$125
Cobalt Blue.	$150-$200	Ivory.	$150-$200
Forest Green.	$250-$300	Medium Green.	$1,600-$1,800
Gray.	$200-$250	Red.	$175-$225

Disk water pitcher in Cobalt Blue.

Disk water pitcher in Green.

Rose. . . . . $275-$325   Yellow. . . . . $110-$140
Turquoise. . . . . $110-$140

Disk water pitcher in Ivory.

Disk water pitcher in Red.

Disk water pitcher in Turquoise.

Disk water pitcher in Medium Green.

Disk water pitcher in Rose.

Disk water pitcher in Turquoise.

Disk water pitcher in Yellow.

Disk water pitchers, right, in vintage Cobalt Blue; left, in Post-'86 Sapphire, sold by Bloomingdale's.

Ice-lip pitcher

Ice-lip pitcher in Turquoise.

Dimensions: 6 3/8" by 9 3/4" by 6 1/2". Produced from 1936 to 1946, it is marked "HLC USA." Production of Red examples was halted in 1944.

Degree of Difficulty: 2-3 for colors other than Red, which ranks 4.

Cobalt Blue, Green, Ivory, Red, Turquoise, and Yellow. . . . . $125-$150

Ice-lip pitcher in Ivory.

Ice-lip pitcher in Yellow.

Two-pint jug

Two-pint jug in Turquoise.

Two-pint jug in Red.

Dimensions: 4 1/4" by 8 1/2" by 5 1/2". Produced from 1936 until 1959, it may be marked "HLC USA" with a "5" near the Fiesta logo, or "Made in USA" without the number. This pitcher had originally been the largest in a proposed series of five in graduated sizes, but it was the only one put into production.

Degree of Difficulty: 2-3

Two-pint jug in Chartreuse.

Two-pint jug in Rose.

Chartreuse, Forest Green, Gray, and Rose. . . . . $125-$150
Cobalt Blue, Ivory, and Red. . . . . $100-$125
Green, Turquoise, and Yellow. . . . . $75-$85

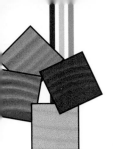

Plates

6" plate

6" plate in Gray.

Also called the bread and butter plate, 6 1/4" diameter. Produced from 1936 to 1969, most have a "Genuine Fiesta" stamp. Production of Red examples was halted in 1944 and resumed in 1959. It is the most common piece of Fiesta found.

Degree of Difficulty: 1

Chartreuse, Cobalt Blue, Forest Green, Gray, Green, Ivory, Red, Rose, Turquoise, and Yellow. . . . . $5-$10
Medium Green. . . . . $25-$35

6" and 7" plates in Red.

6" and 7" plates in Medium Green.

7" *plate*

6" and 7" plates in Ivory.

Actual diameter 7 1/2" Produced from 1936 until 1969, this plate often bears the "Genuine Fiesta" stamp when marked. Production of Red examples was halted in 1944 and resumed in 1959.

Degree of Difficulty: 1

6" and 7" plates in Medium Green.

Chartreuse, Cobalt Blue, Forest Green, Gray, Green, Ivory, Red, Rose, Turquoise, and Yellow. . . . . $8-$12
Medium Green. . . . . $50-$60

9" plate

9" plate in Medium Green. (Note color and ring pattern variation between this and the 10" plate.)

Actual diameter 9 1/2". Produced from 1936 until 1969, this plate often bears the "Genuine Fiesta" stamp when marked. Production of Red examples was halted in 1944 and resumed in 1959.

Degree of Difficulty: 1-2

Chartreuse, Cobalt Blue, Forest Green, Gray, Green, Ivory, Red, Rose, Turquoise, and Yellow. . . . . $15-$25
Medium Green. . . . . $70-$80

*Place setting with 9" plate, teacup, and saucer, and 6" and 7"
plates in Yellow. (Note color differences in smaller plates.)*

Place setting with 9" plate, teacup, and saucer, and 6" and 7" plates in Green.

*Place setting with 9" plate, teacup, and saucer, and 6" and 7"
plates in Red.*

Place setting with 9" plate, teacup, and saucer, and 6" and 7" plates in Cobalt Blue.

Place setting with 9" plate, teacup, and saucer, and 6" and 7" plates in Ivory. (Note color differences in smaller plates.)

Place setting with 9" plate, teacup, and saucer, and 6" and 7" plates in Turquoise. (Note ring pattern variation in large plate.)

Place setting with 9" plate, teacup, and saucer, and 6" and 7" plates in Medium Green.

Place setting with 9" plate, teacup, and saucer, and 6" and 7" plates in Gray.

Place setting with 9" plate, teacup, and saucer, and 6" and 7" plates in Rose.

Place setting with 9" plate, teacup, and saucer, and 6" and 7" plates in Chartreuse.

Place setting with 9" plate, teacup, and saucer, and 6" and 7" plates in Forest Green.

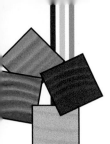

10" *plate*

10" plate in Medium Green.

Actual diameter 10 1/2". Produced from 1935 until 1969, this plate often bears the "Genuine Fiesta" stamp when marked. Production of Red examples was halted in 1944 and resumed in 1959.

Degree of Difficulty: 1-2

10" plate in Cobalt Blue.

Chartreuse, Cobalt Blue, Forest Green, Gray, Green, Ivory, Red, Rose, Turquoise, and Yellow. . . . . $40-$50
Medium Green. . . . . $150-$200

10" plate in Green.

10" plate in Yellow.

10" plate in Ivory.

10" plate in Red.

10" plate in Turquoise.

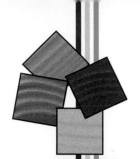

Cake plate

Dimensions: 10 3/8" diameter. Produced for only a matter of months in 1937, some have been found with a "Royal Chrome Colored Ovenware" sticker and may have had a separate pierced metal base. The rings on the bottom are numerous and may have a heavier appearance. The plate is flat and only about 1/2" deep.

Degree of Difficulty: 4-5

Cobalt Blue. . . . . $950-$1,050   Ivory. . . . . $850-$900
Green. . . . . $900-$950   Red. . . . . $1,500+

Calendar plate

Dimensions: 9" and 10" diameter. There is no clear explanation for why these plates were made for only two years. The 1954 plate was 10" in diameter and came only in Ivory. The 1955 plates were either 9" or 10", and came in Light Green, Ivory, and Yellow. None have a manufacturer's mark.

Degree of Difficulty: 2-3

Light Green, Ivory, and Yellow. . . . . . $40-$50

13" Chop plate

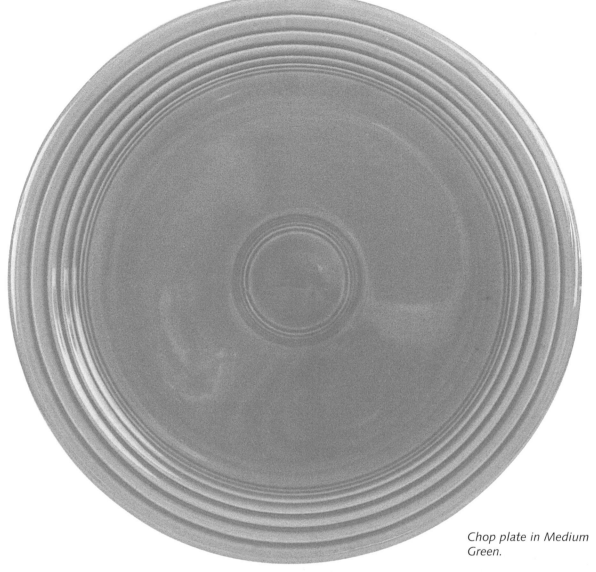

Chop plate in Medium Green.

Actual diameter 12 3/8". These plates were made from 1936 to 1969, and are stamped "Genuine Fiesta," though some are unmarked. They are found with both single and double foot rings, though no one is sure why this occurs. A raffia-wrapped metal handle was offered as a special promotion and could be clipped onto the plate.

Degree of Difficulty: 1-2 for colors other than Medium Green, which ranks 3-4.

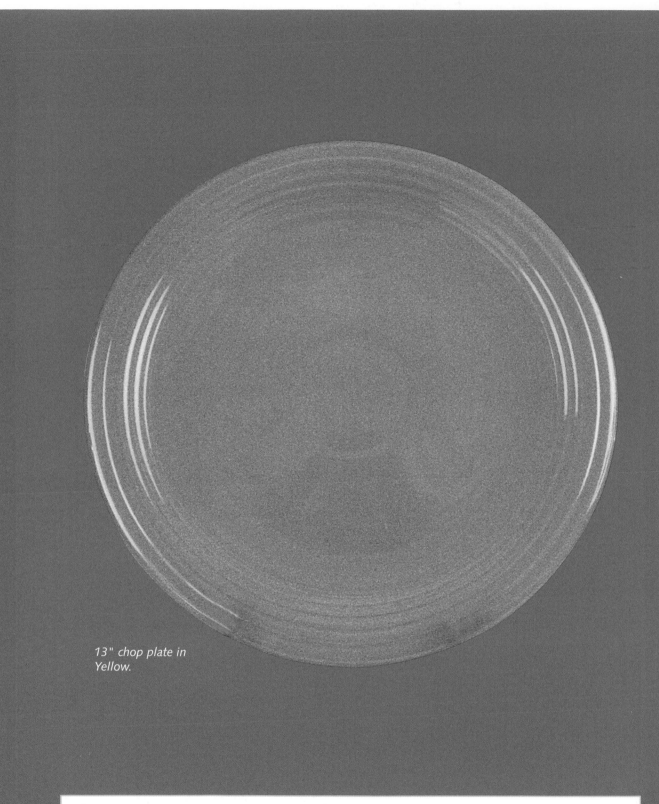

13" chop plate in Yellow.

Chartreuse, Forest Green, Gray, and Rose. . . . .$80-$100
Cobalt Blue, Green, Ivory, Red, Turquoise, and Yellow. . . . .$40-$60
Medium Green. . . . . $600-$700

13" chop plate in Turquoise.

13" chop plate in Rose.

13" chop plate in Green.

13" chop plate in Ivory.

15" Chop plate

15" chop plate in Ivory with Green bud vase.

Actual diameter 14 1/4". Made from 1936 until 1959, they also have a double foot ring and are stamped "Genuine Fiesta." These plates often have significant surface scratching, which is most evident on dark glazes.

Degree of Difficulty: 1-2 for original colors, 2-3 for Fifties colors.

15" chop plate in Red with Yellow bud vase.

Chartreuse, Forest Green, Gray, and Rose. . . . . $150-$175
Cobalt Blue, Green, Ivory, Red, Turquoise, and Yellow. . . . . . $80-$110

15" chop plate in Cobalt Blue with Ivory bud vase.

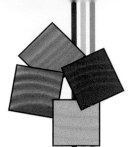

10½" Compartment plate

10 1/2" compartment plate in Red.

Made from 1937 until 1959, this size replaced the 12" version and has slightly deeper compartments. It is routinely stamped "Genuine Fiesta."

Degree of Difficulty: 2

Chartreuse, Forest Green, Gray, and Rose. . . . . $70-$80
Cobalt Blue, Green, Ivory, Red, Turquoise, and Yellow. . . . . . . $35-$50

12" Compartment plate

12" compartment plate in Cobalt Blue.

Actual diameter 11 3/4". Sold for only about 12 months in 1936-37, this size is not marked, and the compartments are slightly shallower than the 10 1/2" size.

Degree of Difficulty: 2

12" compartment plate in Red.

Cobalt Blue, Green, Ivory, Red, and Yellow. . . . . $50-$70

Deep plate

Deep plate in Medium Green

Dimensions: 8 3/8" by 1 3/8". Intended for serving soup, this piece was made from 1936 until 1969, and is stamped "Genuine Fiesta." Production of Red examples was halted in 1944 and resumed in 1959.

Degree of Difficulty: 1-2

Deep plate in Red.

Deep plate in Turquoise.

Chartreuse, Cobalt Blue, Forest Green, Gray, Green, Ivory, Red, Rose, Turquoise, and Yellow. . . . . $40-$65
Medium Green. . . . . $125-$150

Deep plate in Cobalt Blue.

Deep plate in Ivory.

Deep plate in an unusually strong Light Green glaze.

Deep plate in a strong Light Green glaze next to a teacup in Medium Green.

Deep plate in Yellow.

Deep plate in Chartreuse.

Deep plate in Rose.

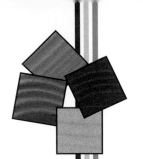

Platters
Oval platter

Oval platter in Medium Green.

Dimensions: 12 3/4" long before 1947; 12 1/2" long after 1947. Produced from 1938 to 1969, it is commonly marked with a "Genuine Fiesta" stamp. Production of Red examples was halted in 1944 and resumed in 1959.

Degree of Difficulty: 2

Oval platter in Cobalt Blue.

Chartreuse, Cobalt Blue, Forest Green, Gray, Green, Ivory, Red, Rose, Turquoise, and Yellow. . . . . $45-$65
Medium Green . . . .$200-$225

Oval platter in Ivory.

Oval platter in Turquoise.

Oval platter in Chartreuse.

Oval platter in Yellow.

Oval platter in Green.

Salt & pepper shakers

Shakers in Medium Green.

Dimensions: 2 3/8" by 2 3/4". Originally available separately and seldom marked, the shakers were sold from 1936 to 1969. They are also available in Fiesta Ironstone and Amberstone colors. But after 1967, the pepper shaker was made with six holes rather than seven. They came with cork stoppers, and like most shakers, the pepper holes are slightly smaller than those for salt. Production of Red examples was halted in 1944 and resumed in 1959.

Degree of Difficulty: 1-2 for colors other than Medium Green, which ranks 3-4.

Shakers in Cobalt Blue.

Chartreuse, Cobalt Blue, Forest Green, Gray, Green, Ivory, Red, Rose, Turquoise, and Yellow.
. . . . . $25-$45/**pair**

Medium Green.
. . . $225-$250/**pair**

Shakers in Yellow.

Shakers in Green.

Shakers in Red.

Shakers in Ivory.

Shakers in Turquoise, note color variation.

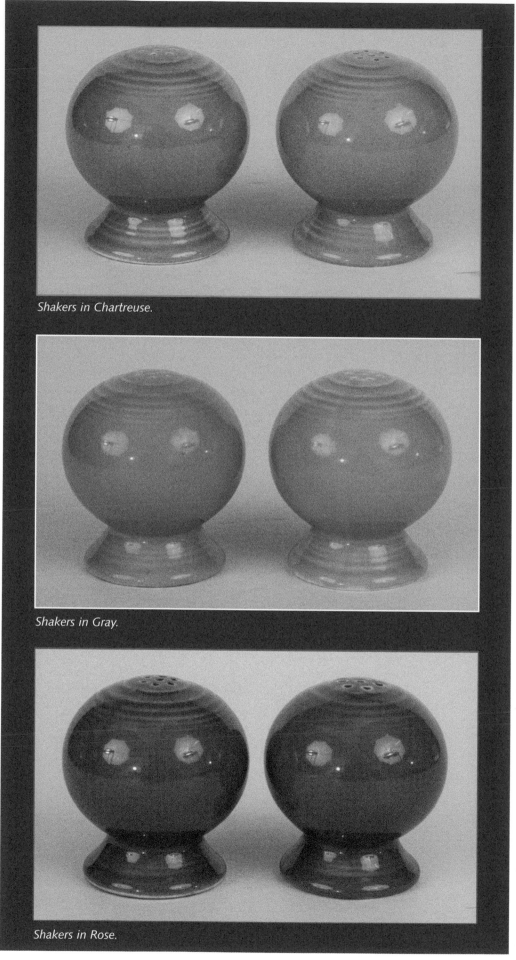

Shakers in Chartreuse.

Shakers in Gray.

Shakers in Rose.

Sauce boat

Sauce boat in Medium Green.

Sauce boat in Medium Green
(shown with covered sugar).

Dimensions: 4 7/8" by 8" by 4 1/2". This piece was part of the vintage line from 1937 to 1969 (marked "Fiesta/HLC U.S.A." or "Fiesta/Made in U.S.A."), and is available in the Ironstone colors (unmarked) and in the Post-'86 line. Production of vintage Red was halted in 1944 and resumed in 1959.

Degree of Difficulty: 1-2 for colors other than Medium Green, which ranks 3-4.

Sauce boat in Cobalt Blue.

Sauce boat and stand in Red.

Chartreuse, Cobalt Blue, Forest Green, Gray, Red, and Rose. . . $70-$80
Green, Ivory, Turquoise, and Yellow . . . . $45-$65
Sauce boat in Medium Green. . . . . $200-$225

Sauce boat in Ivory.

Sauce boat in Yellow.

Sauce boat in Turquoise.

Sauce boat in Gray.

Sauce boat in Forest Green.

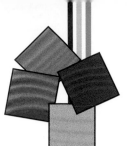

Sugar bowl with lid

Covered sugar in Medium Green.

Also called the covered sugar. Dimensions: 3 3/4" without handles by 5" with lid. Sold from 1936 until 1969, the covered sugar underwent an early design change just months after introduction. The inside bottom was changed from flat to rounded and the lid is slightly shallower. It can be marked either "Fiesta/HLC U.S.A." or "Made in U.S.A." Those in Fifties colors may have a foot that is slightly less flared. Production of Red examples was halted in 1944 and resumed in 1959.

Degree of Difficulty: 1-2 for colors other than Medium Green, which ranks 2-3.

Covered sugar in Medium Green (shown with ring-handle creamer).

Covered sugar and stick-handle creamer in Red.

Chartreuse, Cobalt Blue, Forest Green, Gray, Red, and Rose. . . $60-$70
Green, Ivory, Turquoise, and Yellow. . . . . $45-$60
Medium Green. . . . . $225-$250

Covered sugar in Turquoise.

Covered sugar in Yellow.

Syrup pitcher with "Dripcut" lid

Two syrup pitchers, one in Ivory with a turquoise top marked on the bottom, "Dripcut Heat Proof L.A. Cal.," and one in Red with a red top marked on the bottom, "HLC Fiesta Made in U.S.A."

Dimensions: 5 3/4" including top by 3 5/8" without handle. Produced for only two years, from 1938 to 1940, the plastic and metal Dripcut tops are found in the original six colors, with slight color variations because of age. The pitcher body was also used as a lamp base and as a container for Dutchess Tea.

Degree of Difficulty: 3-4

Dripcut syrup pitcher in Cobalt Blue with a blue top, marked Fiesta.

Cobalt Blue, Green, Ivory,
Red, Turquoise, and Yellow.
. . . . **$350-$450**

Lamp with syrup pitcher body, paper shade, and pot-metal base, 14 in. tall.

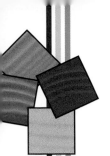

Teapots
Medium teapot

Medium teapot in Medium Green.

Dimensions: 8 1/2" by 5 1/8" with lid, by 5 5/8". Though a small Fiesta teapot was considered for the line, it was never produced. This size differs from the large teapot in its lid finial, which does not flare; the spout, which is longer and arched; and the handle, which is C-shaped, rather than a ring. It was produced from 1937 to 1969, though production of Red examples was halted in 1944 and resumed in 1959.

Degree of Difficulty: 2-3

Medium teapot in Red.

Chartreuse, Cobalt
Blue, Forest Green,
Ivory, Red, and
Rose.
. . . . . **$250-$300**
Gray. . . **$425-$475**
Green, Turquoise,
and Yellow.
. . . . . **$150-$175**
Medium Green.
. . **$1,600-$1,700**

Medium teapot in Ivory.

Medium teapot in Turquoise.

Medium teapot in Yellow.

Medium teapot in Rose.

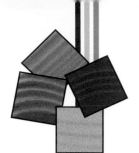

Large teapot

Large teapot in Yellow.

Dimensions: 9 1/4" by 6 3/4" with lid, by 6 1/8". Sold from 1936 until 1946, this may be marked either "Fiesta/HLC USA" or "Made in USA." The lids typically have a steam vent hole.

Degree of Difficulty: 2-3

Cobalt Blue, Green, Ivory, Red, Turquoise, and Yellow. . . . . $300-$400

Trays

Relish tray

Relish tray in Cobalt Blue, Green, Ivory, Red, Turquoise and Yellow.

Tray (relish, with five inserts) overall dimensions: 10 7/8" by 1 1/2". Sold from 1936 to 1946, the tray is typically marked "Fiesta/HLC USA" while the inserts may be unmarked, or marked "Genuine Fiesta/Made in USA." The quarter-round inserts come in two sizes, and when mixed, will not fit snugly around the center section. Production of Red was discontinued in 1944.

Degree of Difficulty: 2-3

Relish tray and inserts in Turquoise, as it would have come from the factory.

Cobalt Blue, Green, Ivory, Red, Turquoise, and Yellow.
. . . . $300-$375/set

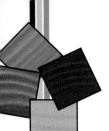

Tidbit tray

Tidbit tray in Ivory, Turquoise, and Cobalt Blue.

Tidbit trays are found in 2- and 3-tier versions in both original and Fifties color variations. There are no official records of HLC making these as actual pieces, but there is evidence it made some of the original holed-plates for construction of the trays. When taken apart, some tray plates can be found with glazed center holes, as they would have come from the factory, while others are clearly drilled post-factory (the hardware was and still is readily available).

Utility tray

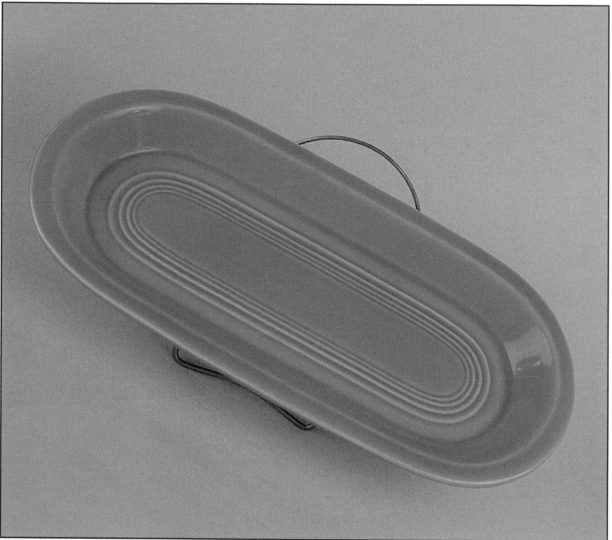

Utility tray in Green.

Dimensions: 10 1/2" by 1 1/4". Made from 1936 to 1946, this tray comes in two varieties: the earlier version has a narrower racetrack base that is not glazed, and the sides have less of a slant; the later version (introduced in 1938) has a wider base that is glazed and is typically marked "Genuine Fiesta/HLC USA." Production of Red examples was halted in 1944.

Degree of Difficulty: 1-2 for later style, 3-4 for earlier style.

Utility tray in Yellow.

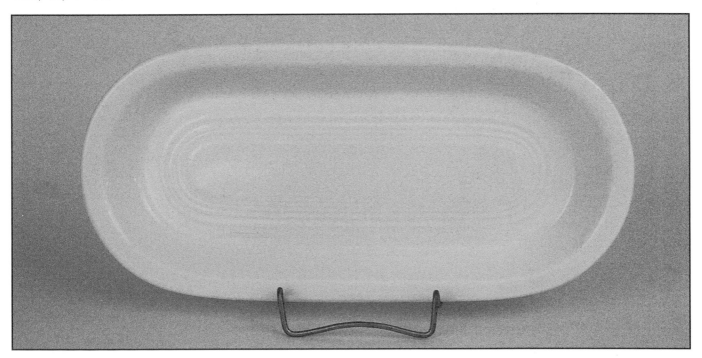

Utility tray in Ivory.

Cobalt Blue, Green, Ivory, Red, Turquoise, and Yellow. . . . . . . $40-$55

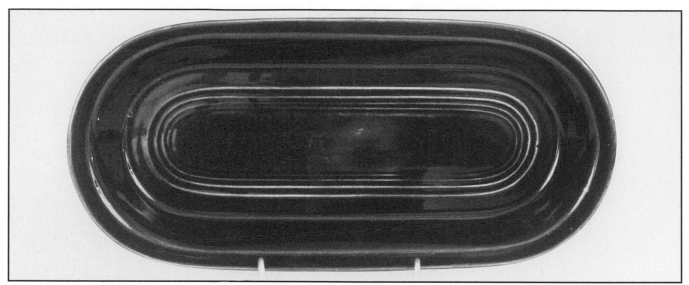

Utility tray in Cobalt Blue.

Utility tray in Turquoise.

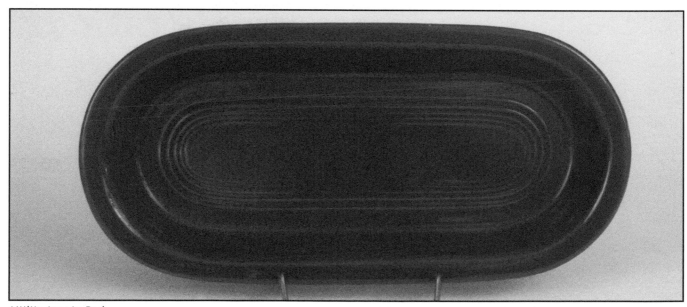

Utility tray in Red.

Tumblers

Juice tumbler

Six Fiesta juice tumblers in Yellow, Turquoise, Red, Cobalt Blue, Ivory, and Green, plus a Fiesta juice tumbler in Harlequin Rose.

Juice tumblers in Chartreuse and Harlequin Yellow, Rose, and Turquoise, with a Red disk juice pitcher.

Dimensions: 3 3/4" or 3 1/2" by 2 1/2". Produced from 1939 until 1943, they were also made for special promotions in 1948 (called "Jubilee"), in about 1951 (for the Woolworth's "Rhythm" line that included Harlequin Yellow), and as a promotion for Old Reliable Coffee. The tumblers were part of a seven-piece set that included the disk juice pitcher in Gray (rare), Red, Turquoise (very rare), and both Fiesta and Harlequin Yellow. Seldom marked, they may have an "HLCo USA" stamp.

Degree of Difficulty: 1-2 for colors other than Chartreuse, Forest Green, and Gray (3-4).

Chartreuse. . . . . $550-$600
Cobalt Blue, Green, Ivory, Red, Rose,
   Turquoise, and Yellow. . . . . $45-$60

Forest Green. . . . . $400-$500
Gray. . . . . $225-$275

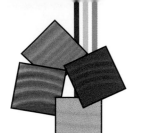

Water tumbler

Three water tumblers in Green, Cobalt Blue, and Turquoise.

Dimensions: 4 1/2" by 3 3/8". Produced from 1937 until 1946, the water tumbler differs from the juice tumbler not only in size, but also in profile, with its more flared mouth. It can be marked either "Fiesta/HLC USA" or "Made in USA." Production of Red examples was halted in 1944. There may be minute variations in height.

Degree of Difficulty: 1-2

Cobalt Blue, Green, Ivory, Red, Turquoise, and Yellow. . . . . . . $70-$90

Vases
Bud vase

Bud vases in Turquoise, Cobalt Blue, Ivory, Yellow, Green, and Red.

Dimensions: 6 1/4" by 2 7/8". Made from 1936 until 1946, this vase is also part of the Post-'86 line, with a minute difference in height, and, of course, color. Vintage pieces may be marked either "Fiesta/HLC USA" or "Made in USA." Production of Red examples was halted in 1944.

Degree of Difficulty: 1-2

Cobalt Blue, Green, Ivory, Red, Turquoise, and Yellow. . . . . **$100-$150**

Bud vases, left, in vintage Yellow; right, in Post-'86 Sunflower.

Bud vases, left, Post-'86 Turquoise; right, vintage Turquoise.

Bud vases, left, Post-'86 Cobalt Blue; right, vintage Cobalt Blue.

Bud vases, left, Post-'86 Persimmon; right, vintage Red.

Vases: 8", 10", 12"

8" vases in Turquoise, Red, and Yellow.

The 10" and 12" sizes were made from 1936 to 1942; the 8" stayed in production until 1946, except for Red examples, which were dropped in 1944. The larger sizes are typically marked "Fiesta/HLC USA," while the 8" may also be marked "Made in USA." There are minute height variations in all three sizes.

Degree of Difficulty: 2-3 depending on color.

Vase 8"

Cobalt Blue, Green, Ivory, Red, Turquoise, and Yellow. . . . . $650-$800

Vase 10"
Cobalt Blue, Green, Ivory, Red,
Turquoise, and Yellow
. . . . $1,000-$1,300

10" vase in Ivory.

Three vases—
8", 10", and 12"—in Red.

Vase 12"

Actual height, about 11 3/4".

Cobalt Blue, Green, Ivory, and Yellow. . . . . $1,100-$1,500
Red. . . . . $1,850-$2,000
Turquoise. . . . . $1,500-$1,600

Left to right: 8", 10", and 12" vases in Turquoise, Yellow, and Cobalt Blue.

Amberstone, Casuals, Casualstone, Ironstone

Amberstone

Fiesta Amberstone marmalade, left, and a Post-'86 standard sugar bowl in Black.

None of the following four lines were intended to have Fiesta stamps, but since some styles and colors were shared, and production times overlapped, a few oddities exist. Some resources also combine the production dates for more than one line, but since each has distinct characteristics, we present them here as separate lines.

Amberstone dinnerwares—in both modified and original Fiesta shapes—were distributed as part of the Sheffield line by J&H International of Wilmette, Ill., beginning in 1967 as a grocery store promotion. The rich, coffee-color glaze can be found on 27 items, from ashtrays to vegetable bowls, and also featured a stylized scroll and shield decoration in black, mostly on plates. Amberstone was produced for about two years.

Degree of Difficulty: 1

Fiesta Amberstone covered butter dish.

Fiesta Amberstone deep plate.

Fiesta Amberstone place setting with 10" plate, cup and saucer, and 6" bread plate.

Casuals

The Casuals line from the mid-1960s featured two patterns—"Yellow Carnation" and "Hawaiian 12-Point Daisy"—on plates that were matched with vintage-style Yellow and Turquoise pieces, respectively. The solid-color matching pieces included the ring-handle creamer, covered sugar, 5 1/2" fruit bowl, 8 1/2" nappy, and the teacup.

Degree of Difficulty: 2-3

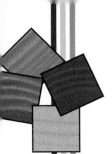

Casualstone

Casualstone place setting with 10" plate, cup and saucer, and 7" plate in Antique Gold.

The Casualstone line from 1970 was another short-lived grocery store promotion, distributed by Coventry Ware of Barberton, Ohio, and stamped "Coventry." It has the Antique Gold glaze and the plates have a stamped pattern of stylized leaves and scrolls. It was made in the same 27 shapes as Amberstone. Design changes include C-handles on the cups and creamer, and a more flared knob on the lids of covered pieces.

Degree of Difficulty: 1

Casualstone 13" chop plate (front and back) in Antique Gold.

Ironstone

Cup and saucer in Turf Green.

Cup and saucer in
Antique Gold.

Fiesta Ironstone was introduced in 1969 with the colors of
Antique Gold, Mango Red (same as original Red), and Turf
Green (olive). The new shapes included a 5 1/2" fruit/dessert
bowl, a 6 1/2" soup/cereal bowl, a 10 1/2" salad bowl, an 8 7/8"
vegetable bowl, a covered casserole (like several other Ironstone
pieces, available only in Antique Gold), a straight-side coffee
mug, a sauceboat underplate or "stand," and a covered sugar
bowl without handles. Other pieces based on vintage shapes also
received restyled knobs and handles, and these design updates
can also be found in Amberstone and Casualstone.

Degree of Difficulty: 2-3

Amberstone Brown fruit/dessert bowl, and two Ironstone fruit/dessert bowls in Turf Green and Antique Gold.

Ironstone soup/cereal bowl in Mango Red.

Ironstone sauceboat stands in Antique Gold, Turf Green, and Mango Red.

Ironstone 7" plate in Turf Green.   *Ironstone 7" plate in Antique Gold.*

Ironstone 10" plate in Antique Gold.

Ironstone 10" plate in Turf Green

Ironstone S&P shakers in Antique Gold, and Amberstone Brown S&P shakers.

Ironstone sauceboat in Turf Green.

Ironstone oval platter in Turf Green.

Ironstone covered sugar in Antique Gold, and a creamer in Antique Gold in original packaging and with store coupon, next to a covered sugar in Amberstone.

Ironstone saucers in Antique Gold and Turf Green in original packaging.

Ironstone 7" plate, and cups in original packaging, all in Turf Green.

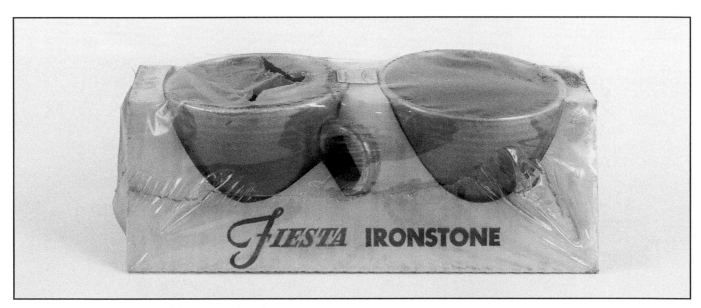

Ironstone cups in Antique Gold, in original packaging.

Striped Fiesta

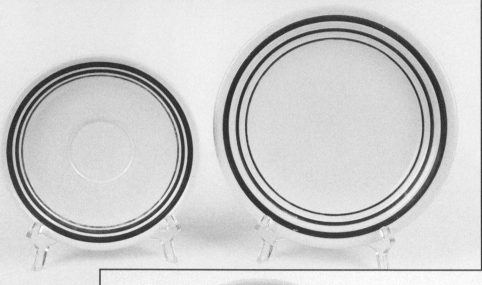

Saucer and 7" plate with three blue stripes.

6" plate and 5 1/2" fruit bowl with red stripes.

Fiesta pieces with stripes came in two styles: the first came near the beginning of production in the late 1930s, and has three concentric rings—in blue and red—around the edges of Ivory pieces that include bowls, casseroles, cups, lids, plates, and saucers. The other style is part of a cake set numbering five or seven pieces sold by Sears during the mid-1940s, and features two bands of color, usually green or maroon, on Ivory and Yellow 10" and 7" plates. These pieces are usually valued at three to four times the price of similar examples without stripes.

Striped plates sold as part of cake sets by Sears, circa 1937: 7" plates in green on Yellow and maroon on Yellow; 10" and 7" plates in green on Ivory.

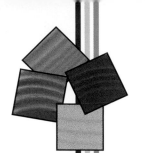

Fiesta Kitchen Kraft

Fiesta Kitchen Kraft salad fork in Green $125 to $140.

Fiesta Kitchen Kraft cake lifter in Cobalt Blue $150 to $160 (shown with salad fork).

Items in the Fiesta Kitchen Kraft line were produced from 1938 to the mid-1940s, in Cobalt Blue, Green, Red, and Yellow, and included 21 pieces. An impressed mark, "Fiesta Kitchen Kraft U.S.A.," and an applied label, "Guaranteed Fiesta Kitchen Kraft U-S-A," were both used. Kitchen Kraft shapes in Fiesta colors were also offered in special promotions for the Royal Metal Manufacturing Co. of Chicago, and in combination with regular Fiesta pieces. Some items are not difficult to find, but those with original labels bring a premium.

Fiesta Kitchen Kraft individual casserole in Green $150 to $160.

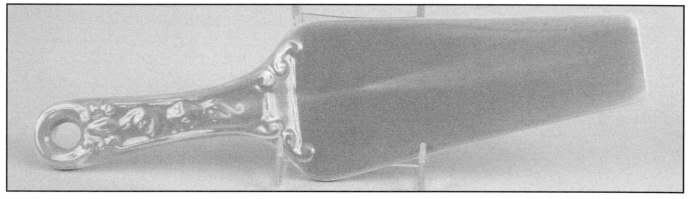

Fiesta Kitchen Kraft cake lifter in Yellow $140 to $150.

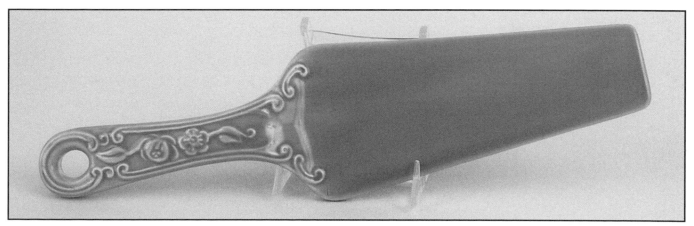

Fiesta Kitchen Kraft cake lifter in Green $140 to $150.

Fiesta Kitchen Kraft shakers in Green and Cobalt Blue $90 to $110.

Fiesta Kitchen Kraft shakers in Red $90 to $110 pair.

Fiesta Kitchen Kraft refrigerator sets, with three bodies in Green, Cobalt Blue, and Ivory $45 to $55 each, and two covers in Cobalt Blue and Red $75 to $85 each.

Royal Metal pie plate in Fiesta Red with metal stand $60 to $70 pair.

Fiesta Kitchen Kraft cake plate in Yellow $50 to $60.

Two Fiesta Kitchen Kraft covered jars, medium (7 in. diameter) $250 to $300, and large (8 in. diameter) $300 to $350 in Green, the smaller with original label.

Fiesta Kitchen Kraft medium covered jar in Yellow $250 to $300.

Fiesta Kitchen Kraft cake plate in Cobalt Blue $60 to $70.

Fiesta Kitchen Kraft covered casserole in Green $80 to $110.

Fiesta Kitchen Kraft individual casseroles in Green and Yellow $150 to $160 each.

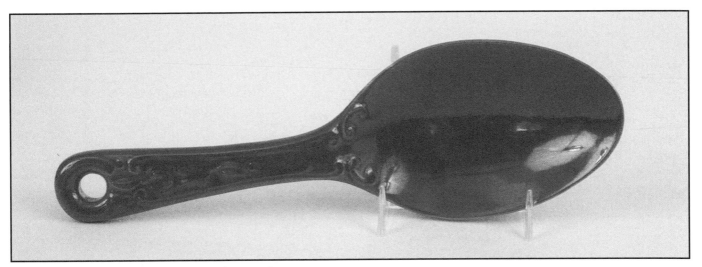

Fiesta Kitchen Kraft salad spoon in Red $140 to $150.

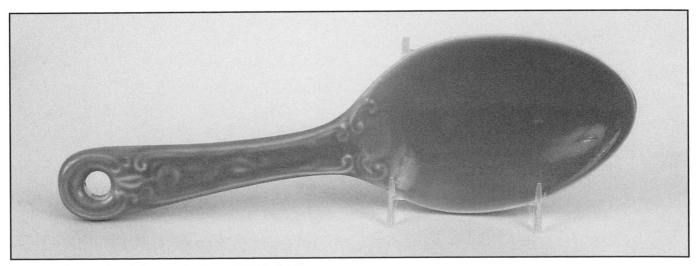

Fiesta Kitchen Kraft salad spoon in Green $125 to $140.

Kitchen Kraft covered casserole in Cobalt Blue on a Royal Chrome stand $130 to $140 pair.

Pie plate in blue, part of the Zephyr line made by Cronin China Co., Minerva, Ohio, in the 1930s.

Kitchen Kraft 9 1/2" pie plate in Fiesta Yellow, left, and 9 1/2" yellow pie plate, part of the Zephyr line made by Cronin China Co., Minerva, Ohio, in the 1930s. (Note difference in rim width.)

9 1/2" pie plates in colors similar to Green and Cobalt Blue, but actually part of the Zephyr line made by Cronin China Co., Minerva, Ohio, in the 1930s.

Post '86
Fiesta Pieces

Fiesta returns

When Homer Laughlin reintroduced the updated Fiesta line on Feb. 28, 1986, a design that had been regarded as tired and outdated in the early 1970s was now seen as ripe with nostalgic appeal. Several Post-'86 items still use vintage mold shapes, including the two larger sizes of the disk pitchers, the sugar/creamer/tray set, the tripod and round candleholders, the C-handle creamer, the sauceboat, the 8" vase, and the salt and pepper shakers.

As with the vintage line, Homer Laughlin also licensed several companies to produce coordinating items for Post-'86 Fiesta, including cutlery, drawer pulls, glassware, kitchen timers, and even message boards.

Homer Laughlin continues to introduce new colors and items to the line, so check with local retailers.

Fiesta colors produced since 1986

Apricot—moderate, pale pink (discontinued in 1998)

Black

Chartreuse—richer, more yellow than the original (discontinued in 1999)

Cinnabar—burgundy or maroon (introduced in 2000)

Cobalt—very dark navy, almost black

Juniper—dark, bluish green (produced from 1999 to 2001)

Lilac—pastel purple or violet (produced from 1993 to 1995)

Pearl Gray—similar to vintage gray, more luminous (produced from 1998 to 2001)

Periwinkle Blue—grayish blue (introduced in 1989)

Persimmon—salmon or coral (introduced in 1995)

Plum—deep purple (introduced in 2002)

Rose—dull, bubblegum pink (it was scheduled for discontinuation in 2002; Homer Laughlin decided to keep it in production, in part because of collector requests)

Sapphire—royal blue (sold only by Bloomingdale's in 1996 and 1997)

Sea Mist Green—pastel, light green (introduced in 1991)

Shamrock—dark, grassy green (introduced in 2003)

Sunflower—bright, rich yellow (introduced in 2001)

Tangerine—bright orange (introduced in 2003)

Turquoise—greenish blue (introduced in 1988)

White

Yellow—pale yellow, like butter (produced from 1987 to 2002)

Post-'86 items

Bowls: Bouillon, 6 3/4 ounce; Chili, 18 ounce; Fruit, 5 3/8" diameter; Gusto, 23 ounce; Large, 8 1/4" diameter; Medium, 6 7/8" diameter; Mixing (7 1/2", 8 1/2" 9 1/2" diameters); Pasta, 12" diameter; Pedestal, 9 7/8" diameter; Rim Soup, 9" diameter; Small, 5 5/8" diameter; Vegetable (2-quart), 8 1/4" diameter.

Bread Tray, 12" by 5 3/4".

Carafe with Handle, 60 ounce.

Covered Butter, 7 1/8" long.

Covered Casserole, 70 ounce.

Covered Sugar.

Creamer.

Cups: After Dinner ("AD"), 3 ounce; Jumbo, 18 ounce; Regular, 7 3/4 ounce.

Deep Dish Pie Baker, 10 1/4" diameter.

Disc Pitcher: Large, 67 1/4 ounce; Small, 28 ounce; Mini, 5 ounce.

Hostess Tray, 12 1/4" diameter.

Mugs: Cappucino, 21 ounce; Pedestal, 18 ounce; Regular, 10 1/4 ounce.

Oval Platter: 9 5/8" long; 11 5/8" long; 13 5/8" long.

Oval Serving Dish, 12" by 9 1/8".

Plates: Bread and butter, 6 1/8" diameter; Chop, 11 3/4" diameter; Dinner, 10 1/2" diameter; Luncheon, 9" diameter; Pizza, 15" diameter; Salad, 7 1/4" diameter; Snack with well, 10 1/2" diameter.

Relish Tray, 9 1/2 ounce.

Round Candleholder, 3 5/8" tall.

Salt & Pepper: Range set; Round set, each 2 1/5" by 2 5/8".

Sauceboat, 18 1/2 ounce.

Saucers: After Dinner ("AD"), 4 7/8" diameter; Jumbo, 6 3/4" diameter; Regular, 5 7/8" diameter.

Spoon Rest.

Sugar and Creamer Set, 4 pieces including figure-8 tray.

Sugar Packet Holder.

Teapots: Covered, 44 ounce; Two-Cup.

Tool Crock.

Trivet.

Tumblers, 6 1/2 ounce.

Vases: Bud, 6" tall; Medium (called the 10"), 9 5/8" tall; Small, 8" tall, plus the Millennium I, II and III.

Most of the values for Post-'86 Fiesta wares remain at current levels for colors that have not been discontinued, so check with your local retailers or Internet resources for the best prices. Values for some Post-'86 Fiesta wares in discontinued colors have seen dramatic increases, as have those sold only through selected retailers, or pieces with customized decoration. Prices for some new wares now rival those of vintage Fiesta, so check with trusted collectibles dealers (including those listed on our "Resources" page) for the best values in your area.

Place setting with 10" plate, 7" plate and cup and saucer in Lilac.

Three Post-'86 pitchers—disk water, disk juice and mini —in Lilac.

Standard sugar bowl and Fiesta Mates 5-ounce creamer in Black.

Fiesta advertising plate, 12" diameter chop, with Mango Red logo and type.

Millennium I vase in Yellow.

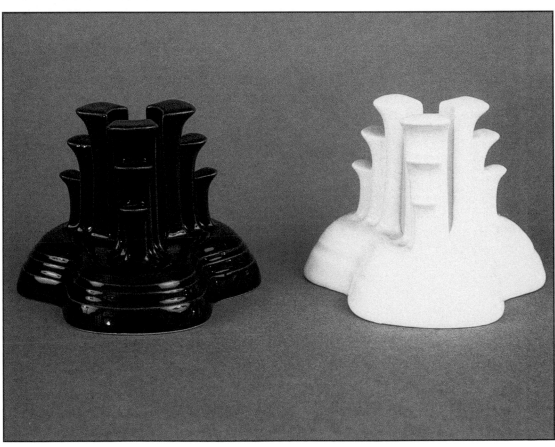

Tripod candleholders in Black and White.

Bread tray and cereal bowl in Yellow.

Millennium
candlesticks
in Yellow.

Spoon rest in Sunflower.

Bouillon cups in Black and White.

Millennium III vase in Persimmon.

Millennium II vase in Turquoise.

10" vase in Lilac.

Vases: two 8" in Cinnabar (left) and Turquoise, and a 10" in Juniper.

Sugar/creamer/figure-8 tray set (made from the original molds) in Lilac.

Carafe and four tumblers in Chartreuse.

Napkin ring set in Persimmon

Commemorative presentation bowl sitting on an upside-down hostess bowl, both in Persimmon, forming a large compote.

Hostess bowl in Persimmon.

Top and bottom
of presentation bowl
(in Persimmon) marking the
500,000,000th piece of Fiesta.

Top and bottom of presentation
bowl (in Chartreuse) marking the 500,000,000th
piece of Fiesta.

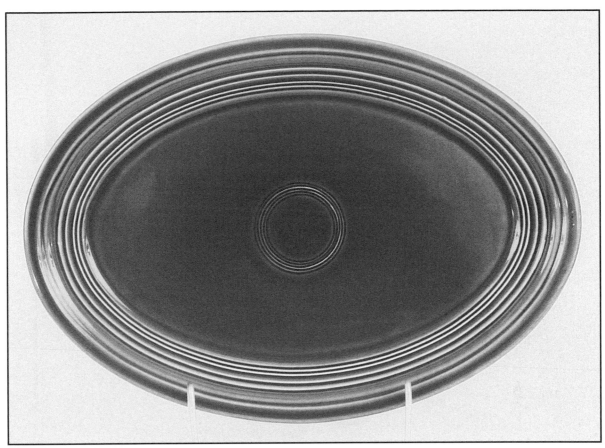

Large platter (13 1/2" wide) in Cobalt Blue.

Two smaller platters in Chartreuse and Turquoise.

Two sizes of pie bakers in Persimmon and Turquoise.

Soup bowl in Juniper and cereal bowl in Turquoise.

Relish or utility in Cobalt Blue.

Fruit bowl in Chartreuse.

Deep plates in Turquoise and Apricot.

Round serving tray in Sapphire.

Tea server in Black, and 2-cup teapot in Persimmon (note difference in handles).

2-cup teapot in Chartreuse.

Trivets in Cobalt and Sunflower.

Sugar and creamer on figure-8 tray in Turquoise.

Covered casserole in Apricot.

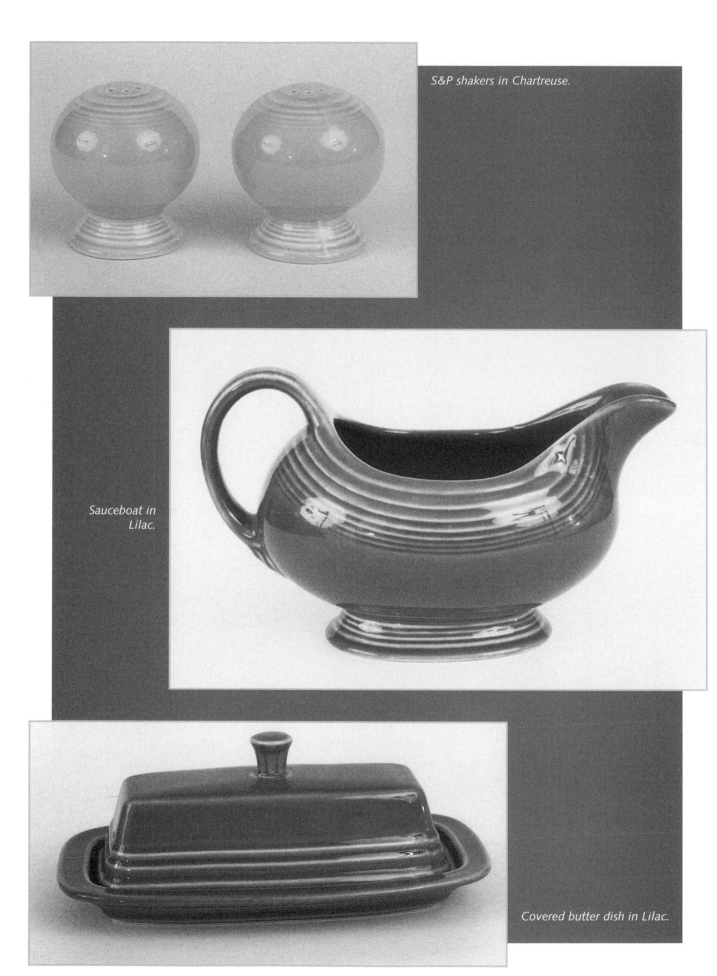

S&P shakers in Chartreuse.

Sauceboat in Lilac.

Covered butter dish in Lilac.

Tom & Jerry mug in Lilac.

Chop plate in Lilac.

Soup bowl and cereal bowl in Lilac.

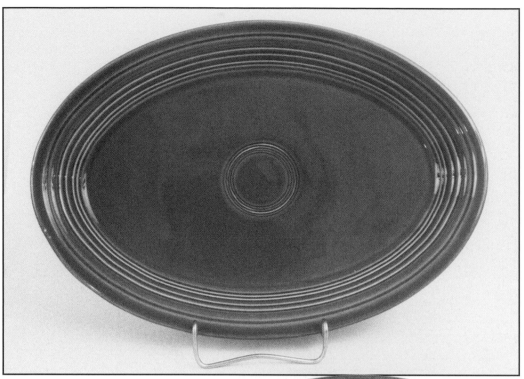

Large oval platter in Lilac.

Pizza tray in Persimmon with glaze flaw.

Hostess tray in Turquoise.

Chili bowl in Persimmon.

Jumbo mug and saucer in Turquoise.

2-quart extra large bowl in Pearl Gray.

10" plate, cup and saucer, 7" plate and soup bowl in Sapphire.

8 1/4" serving bowl in Sapphire.

Round candleholders in Black.

Cereal bowl and 7" plate in Black.

Deep dish casse-role in Turquoise.

Bud vases in Cinnabar, Chartreuse, Persimmon, Turquoise, and Black.

Bud vases in Pearl Gray, Lilac, Plum, Juniper, and Cobalt.

Bud vases in Yellow, White, Sea Mist, Apricot, and Sunflower.

Tom & Jerry mugs in Chartreuse, Sunflower, Shamrock, Cinnabar, Rose, Sea Mist, and Plum.

Tom & Jerry mugs in Persimmon, White, Pearl Gray, Lilac, Juniper, and Turquoise. (One of these is also called the "Fan" or "Horizon" mug.)

Tom & Jerry mug in Persimmon, 60th anniversary.

Tripod bowls in Chartreuse and Juniper.

Disk water pitcher in White with Mickey Mouse.

Goblet in White.

Warner Bros. pie baker in Yellow.

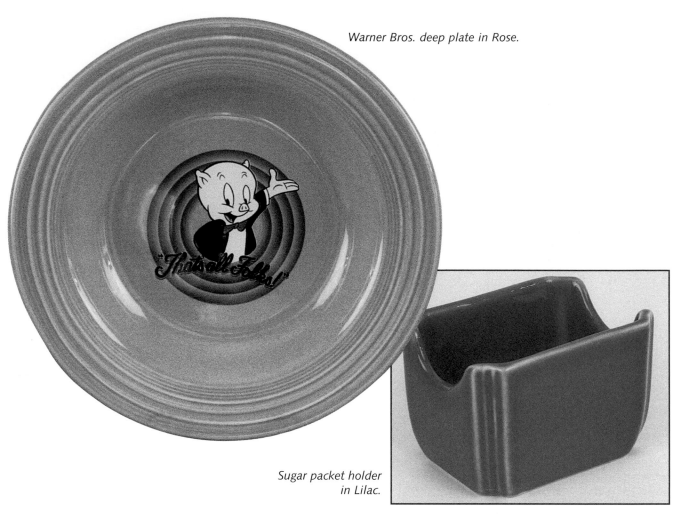

Warner Bros. deep plate in Rose.

Sugar packet holder in Lilac.

Latte cups on Persimmon and Pearl Gray.

Left, cappuccino mug in Cinnabar; right, latte cup in Pearl Gray.

Goblet and fan mug in Persimmon.

Fiesta 2000 round platter, 14 1/2" diameter, and luncheon plate in Pearl Gray; and close-up showing Fiesta 2000 logo.

Fiesta 2000 10" dinner plate in Persimmon, and the all-purpose bowl in Cobalt Blue.

Bud vase in Cobalt Blue with floral decal, and a tumbler in Black with the "Moon Over Miami" decal.

White disk juice pitcher with "Sun Porch" decal, and White tumbler with "Mexicana" decal.

White 9" plate with Millennium decal sold by Federated Department Stores.

Three sizes of mixing bowls in Chartreuse (note color variation).

Three sizes of mixing bowls in Juniper.

Medium bowl and ramekin in Shamrock.

1999 Christmas ornaments in White and Persimmon decorated and signed by former Homer Laughlin art director Jonathan Parry (1948-2000).

Original Post-'86 demitasse cup and saucer in Yellow (redesigned in 2001), and mini disk pitcher in Black with trial decal.

Child's set, including tumbler, bowl and 9" plate with Noah's Ark decal.

Smiling face 9" plate in Sunflower.

"My First Fiesta" set, including 2-cup teapot in Yellow, two ring-handle cups with saucers in Periwinkle and Rose, two 6" plates in Yellow, and a creamer and covered sugar in Turquoise; with original box.

Welled snack plate in Juniper with a White bouillon cup.

Gusto bowl in Sunflower.

Tool crocks in Juniper and Sunflower.

Pedestal bowl in Cobalt Blue.

Ramekins in Apricot, Shamrock, Cobalt Blue, and Cinnabar.

Fiesta clock in Chartreuse (sold only for a matter of months by JC Penney.)

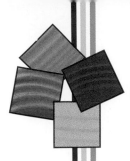

Commemoratives, Souvenirs

White tool crock and small pie baker with Homer Laughlin China Collector's Association 2002 Conference decals.

As with any group of collecting enthusiasts, the Homer Laughlin China Collectors Association holds annual conferences and issues commemorative pieces to mark the occasions. Formed in 1998 as an all-volunteer, member-operated organization, HLCCA is dedicated to providing education and communication for all those interested in the wares of the Homer Laughlin China Co., from 1873 to the present. The Dish, the official publication of HLCCA, is published quarterly.

Homer Laughlin China Collector's Association disk juice pitchers: The 1930 Chrysler Building pitcher was issued in 1999; the 1931 Dick Tracy pitcher was issued in 2000; the 1932 radio pitcher was also issued in 2000; 1933 zeppelin motif was issued in 2001; the 1934 ship design was issued in 2002.

Two mugs with the Ms. Bea decal, from 1999 and 2000; commemorative plate from the 2001 HLCCA conference.

Presentation bowl in Cobalt Blue, gilded for use as the HLCCA exhibition Grand Award and bearing a facsimile of Jonathan Parry's signature, presented to Fred Mutchler.

Disk water pitchers in Cobalt Blue, presented as HLCCA awards to Fred Mutchler in 1999 and 2000, each with a facsimile of the signature of Frederick H. Rhead, original designer of the Fiesta line.

Homer Laughlin Fiesta souvenir plate, 6 1/4" diameter.

Right, 2001 HLCCA Silver Award in a Fiesta disk juice pitcher in Pearl Gray; left, 2002 HLCCA Gold Award in a disk water pitcher in Cobalt Blue.

Fiesta 60th anniversary beverage set: disk water pitcher and four tumblers in Lilac, all with the anniversary mark.

Fiesta Club of America round serving tray in Chartreuse, from 1998. (This group was active for about five years—1995 to 1999—and issued decal trays annually. The first, in Lilac, is valued at about $300-$350.)

50th anniversary (1986) ring-handle mugs, 3 1/4" tall, in White, each having the anniversary sticker.

Fiesta 60th anniversary beverage set: disk water pitcher and four tumblers in Sapphire, all with the anniversary mark, sold by Bloomingdale's.

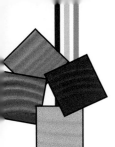

Fiesta Go-Alongs

Four individual salt & pepper shakers, and a "coaster" ashtray, which came with a circa 1941 "All Fiesta Ensemble."

The term "go-alongs" refers to items made to coordinate with both vintage and Post-'86 Fiesta colors. We present a sampling of vintage items here. Examples include flatware, glasses, metal holders, and accessories, even linens and kitchen storage pieces like bread boxes and trash cans.

Go-along glassware with Mexican motifs referred to as the cactus, pot, and sombrero. $15-$20 each

Go-along glassware with banded tops. $10-$15 each

Go-along glassware from the original four-place ensemble in 1939, also called "the dancing lady" ensemble because it includes the only appearance on glass of the Fiesta dancing lady. Rare. $60-$70 each

A collection of go-along utensils made by Sta-Brite Corp., New Haven, Conn., with color-matched handles; the blue handles often turn a purple-black hue.

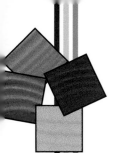

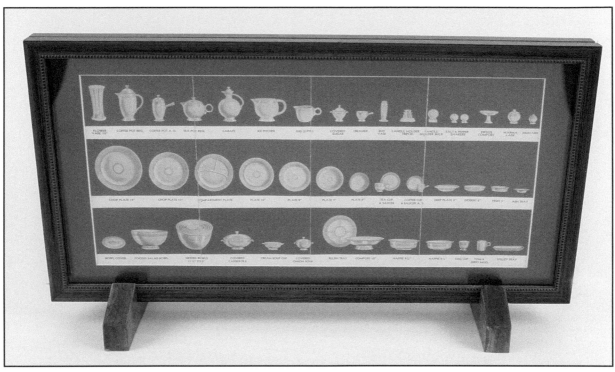

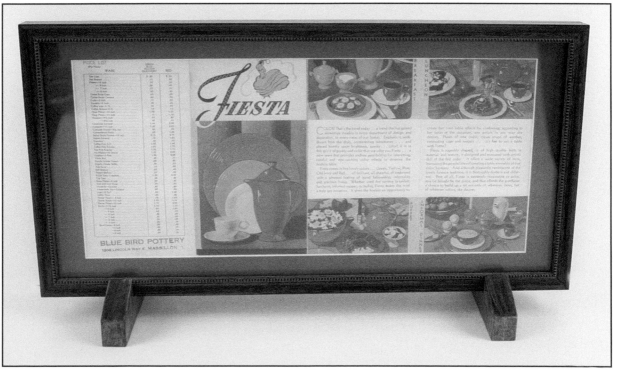

Rare Fiesta advertising brochure, circa 1937, showing the mixing bowl lids, which were produced for only a matter of months.

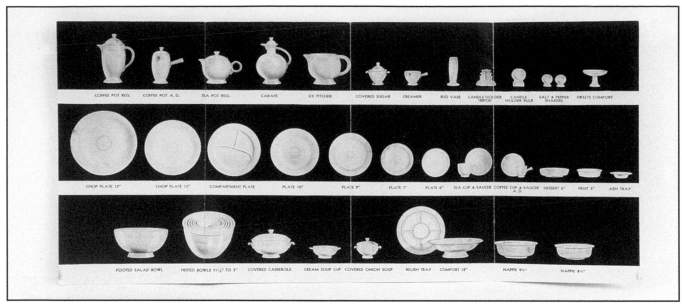

Fiesta advertising brochure, circa 1938, which does not show the mixing bowl lids. (Some brochures for retailers west of the Rocky Mountains have prices that are slightly higher, reflecting the cost of shipping.)

Front and back of a Fiesta promotional poster, circa 1936, showing what may be the first appearance of the dancing lady that became part of the line's logo.

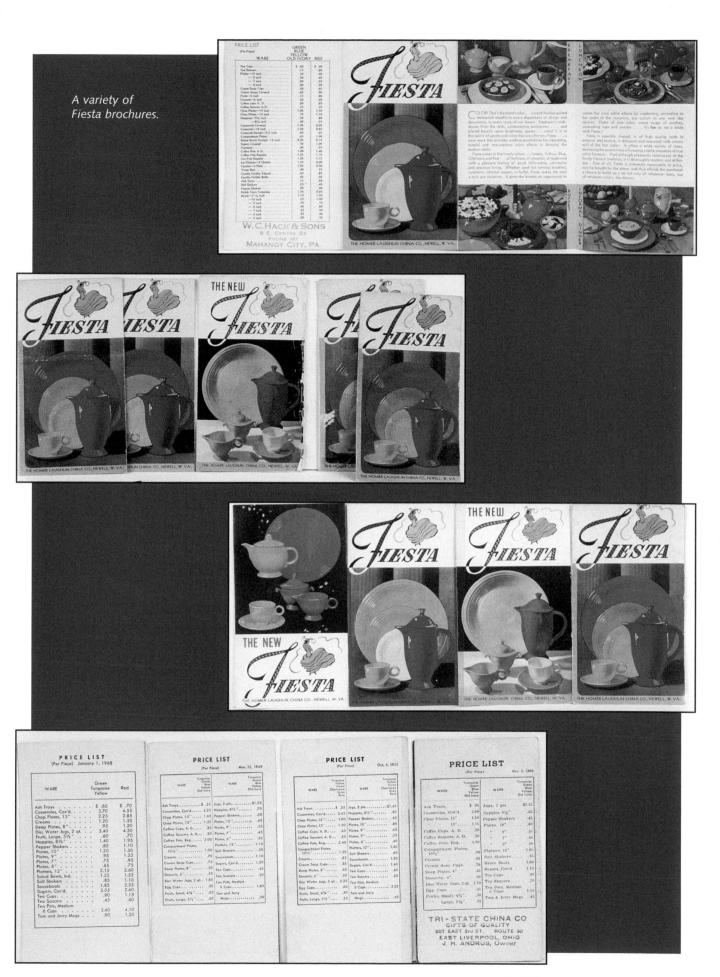

A variety of
Fiesta brochures.

Newspaper ads for Fiesta; some also include other Homer Laughlin products.

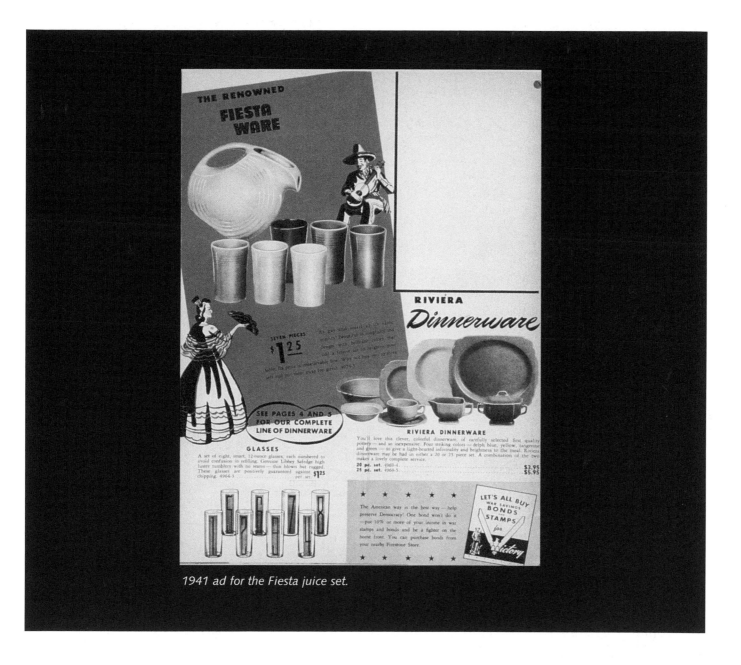

1941 ad for the Fiesta juice set.

Resources

http://mediumgreen.com/ — A message board and collector resource.

The Homer Laughlin China Collectors Association. HLCCA is a non-profit organization comprised of collectors, antiques dealers, historians, etc., who share an interest in the dinnerware and other pottery products produced by the Homer Laughlin China Co. — http://www.hlcca.org/

http://www.gofiesta.net/ — Operated by Fred Mutchler of St. Louis Park, Minn., a six-time HLCCA award winner.

The Homer Laughlin China Co. — http://hlchina.com/

http://www.fiestafanatic.com/ — A portal for books, related items, and Fiesta old and new.

Old Home Antiques — Jim and Jan Van Hoven, Scandia, Minn., (651) 433-2185, JVHFiesta@aol.com

Carlson's Antiques, Bill and Sliv Carlson, Wayzata, Minn., (952) 475-0586, Bill@CarlsonsAntiques.com

Marv and Deb McNuss, Blaine, Minn., (763) 755-6291, mofiesta@aol.com

Ed and Carol Peek, Brooklyn Center, Minn., (763) 535-2919.